P9-DXM-220

TWINS

And What They Tell Us about Who We Are

Lawrence Wright

John Wiley & Sons, Inc.
NEW YORK • CHICHESTER • WEINHEIM • BRISBANE
SINGAPORE • TORONTO

This book is printed on acid-free paper. ♾

...97 by John Wiley & Sons, Inc.

...blished in different form in
...hich first appeared in the
...

...by Weidenfeld & Nicolson

Library of Congress Cataloging-in-Publication Data
Wright, Lawrence
Twins : and what they tell us about who we are / Lawrence Wright.
p. cm.
Includes bibliographical references.
ISBN 0-471-25220-4 (hardcover : alk. paper)
1. Twins—Psychology. 2. Nature and nurture. I. Title.
BF723.T9W75 1998
155.44'4—dc21 97-38827

Printed in the United States of America

10 9 8 7 6 5 4 3 2 1

Contents

ACKNOWLEDGMENTS v

1 Two Lives—One Personality? 1
2 The Nature-Nurture Wars 10
3 The Secret Study 35
4 The Minnesota Experience 43
5 The Critics Respond 67
6 Twin Mysteries 85
7 The Same, but Different 105
8 The Emotional Life 123
9 The Environment We Make 131
10 Beyond Nature versus Nurture 143

BIBLIOGRAPHY 161
INDEX 197

Acknowledgments

It is a pleasure to have the opportunity to thank the many people who contributed their time and energy to making this book. I am particularly grateful to the scientists who are frequently quoted here; contrary to the usual bitter truce that exists between science and the media, many of the most distinguished figures in their fields placed their time and trust in my hands. I hope they will feel rewarded by their efforts.

Much of this book originally appeared in the *New Yorker* magazine, and I wish to extend my deep appreciation to Robert Vare, my editor on this and many other articles and my dear friend as well.

I want to extend particular thanks to Thomas J. Bouchard Jr. and his colleagues at the Minnesota Center for Twin and Adoption Research, who spent many hours patiently responding to my queries. Nancy Segal made innumerable generous suggestions and provided invaluable assistance. In addition, everyone with an interest in twin statistics owes a debt to the peerless "Miss Helen"—Helen Kirk, the unofficial archivist of multiple births. I also want to thank the following people who provided vital information in the preparation of this book: Nicholas Fisk, Elizabeth Noble, Louis

Keith, Donald Keith, Phyllis Markuson Keith, Helain Landy, David Teplica, John Burn, Elizabeth Bryan, Judith Hall, Elena Lopez, Emmanuel Lewis, Judith Goodship, Charles Boklage, Jason Birnholz, Debbie Ganz, Lisa Ganz, Lindon Eaves, Claire Kellman, David Kellman, Robert Shafran, Leon Kamin, Jim Springer, Kay Cassill, Jonathan Marks, Kathryn Roeder, Richard Lewontin, Ashley Montagu, Samuel Abrams, Richard J. Rose, Richard C. Pillard, Arthur Jensen, Evan S. Balaban, Lee Willerman, David Lykken, Tanya Lundgren, Tina Lundgren, Sandra Scarr, Laura Baker, Peter B. Neubauer, Alexander Neubauer, Wai Han Mak, Ken Kendler, Toni Miles, Caryn Carlson, Jack Yufe, Devra Yufe Gregory, Janice Bleyl, Dan Kee, Viola Bernard, J. David Smith, and Juko Ando.

In addition to providing thoughtful insight in the preparation of this book, Ricardo Ainslie, Thomas Mack, and John Loehlin read the manuscript and kept me from making many needless errors. Those that may remain are my responsibility.

Peter Ermey undertook the onerous task of compiling the boxes of research into a coherent bibliography. As usual, Jan McInroy cast her scrupulous eye over the text.

Finally, I wish to thank Ravi Mirchandani, the editor of this book, who recognized the possibility for a larger work and provided invaluable encouragement and guidance.

I

Two Lives—One Personality?

A pair of identical twin girls were surrendered to an adoption agency in New York City in the late 1960s. The twins, who are known in psychological literature as Amy and Beth, might have gone through life in obscurity had they not come to the attention of Dr. Peter Neubauer, a prominent psychiatrist at New York University's Psychoanalytic Institute and a director of the Freud Archives. Neubauer believed at the time that twins posed such a burden to parents, and to themselves in the form of certain developmental hazards, that adopted twins were better off being raised separately, with no knowledge of their twinship.

Neubauer also recognized the exceptional research possibilities such a separation offered. Studies of twins reared apart are one of the most powerful tools that scholars have to analyze the relative contributions of heredity and environment to the makeup of individual human natures. Identical twins are rare, however, and twins who have been separated and brought up in different families are particularly unusual. Neubauer was aware of a mere handful of studies examining twins reared apart, and in most cases the twins being studied had been separated for only part of their childhoods and were reunited at some point long before the study began. Here was an opportunity to look at twins from the moment they were separated, and to trace them through childhood, observing at each stage of development the parallel or diverging courses of their lives. Because the sisters shared the same genetic makeup, one could evaluate the environmental effects on the twins' personalities, their behavior, their health, their intelligence. Such a study might not set to rest the ancient quarrel over the relative importance of nature versus nurture, but there were few other experiments one could imagine that would be more pertinent to an understanding of the human condition. 

Neubauer sought out other instances in which newborn twins were being placed for adoption, eventually adding three other pairs of identical twins and a set of identical triplets to his project. The complete study has never been published, and Neubauer is reluctant to discuss the details of how he enlisted twins into the project. Indeed, much of the history of the study has been kept secret. In any case, by the time that Amy and Beth were sent to their adoptive homes, there was already an extensive team of psychologists, psychiatrists, pediatricians, observers, and testers waiting to follow them as they moved from infancy to adolescence. Every step of childhood would be documented through psychological and ability tests, school records, parental and sibling interviews, films, and the minutes of nearly 1,000 weekly conferences. Not surprisingly, the study was slanted toward psychoanalytical concerns. "In particular, we were looking for the psychological variables which influence developmental processes," says Neubauer. One would expect identical children placed in separate environments to be formed by different family dynamics. Broadly speaking, the personality differences between

the girls as they grew older would measure the validity of the most fundamental assumption of clinical psychology, which is that experience—and, in particular, our family background—shapes us into the people we become.

The agency that placed the children shortly after their birth informed the potential adoptive parents that the girls were already involved in a study of child development, and the parents were strongly urged to continue it; however, neither the parents nor the girls themselves would ever be told that they were twins.

The sisters were fair-skinned blondes with small oval faces, blue-gray eyes, and slightly snub noses. Amy was three ounces heavier and half an inch taller than Beth at birth, an advantage in weight and height that persisted throughout their childhood. The girls were adopted into families that were, in certain respects, quite similar. They were placed in Jewish homes in New York State. The mothers stayed at home, and in each family there was a son almost exactly seven years older than the twin. (In Beth's family, there was an older sister as well.) In other respects, the environments were profoundly different: notably, Amy's family was lower class and Beth's was well off. Amy's mother was overweight and socially awkward. Her personality was flat and her self-esteem was low. Although she had a compassionate side to her nature, she was an insecure mother who felt threatened by her daughter's attractiveness. Beth's mother, on the other hand, doted on her daughter and for the entire ten years of the study spoke positively of Beth's personality and her place in the family. The team described Beth's mother as pleasant, youthful, slim, chic, poised, self-confident, dynamic, and cheerful. Whereas Amy's mother seemed to regard Amy as a problem, a stubborn outsider, Beth's mother treated her daughter as "the fun child." Instead of separating Beth from other members of the family, Beth's mother went out of her way to minimize the differences, to the extent of dyeing her own hair to emphasize their similarities. The girls' fathers were very much like each other—confident, relaxed, at ease with themselves—but different in their treatment of the girls. Amy's father came to agree with his wife that Amy was a disappointment, whereas Beth's father was more available and supportive. Amy's brother was a handsome academic star, the golden boy of the family. Beth's brother, however, was a disturbed child who suffered from learning disabilities and uncontrolled behavior that got him expelled from several schools and in trouble with the law. All in all, the research team characterized Amy's family as a well-knit threesome—mother, father, and son—plus an alienated Amy. It was a family that placed a high value on academic success, simplicity, tradition, and emotional restraint. Beth's family, on the other hand, was sophisticated, full of energy—"frenetic" at times—and it tended to put more emphasis on materialism than on education. Clearly, Beth was more at the center of her home than Amy was in hers.

And how did these identical twins in such contrasting environments turn out? As might be expected, Amy's problems began early and progressed in a disturbing direction. As an infant, she was tense and demanding. She sucked her thumb; she bit her nails; she clung to her blanket; she cried when left alone. She wet her bed until she was four and continued to have "accidents" for several years more. She was prone to nightmares and full of fears. By the age of ten, when the study concluded, she had developed a kind of artificial quality that manifested itself in role-playing, gender confusion, and invented illnesses. Shy, indifferent, suffering from a serious learning disorder, pathologically immature, she was a stereotypical picture of a rejected child. The team proposed that if only Amy had had a mother who had been more empathetic, more tolerant of her limitations, more open and forthcoming (like Beth's mother), then Amy's life might have turned out far better. If only her father had been more consistently available and affectionate (like Beth's father), then she might have been better able to negotiate the oedipal dramas of childhood and achieve a clearer picture of her own sexual role. If only her brother had been less strongly favored (like Beth's brother), Amy would have been spared the mortifying comparisons that were openly drawn in her family. In theory, if Amy had been raised in Beth's family, the sources of her crippling immaturity would have been erased, and she would have been another kind of person—happier, one presumes, and more nearly whole.

In nearly every respect, however, Beth's personality followed in lockstep with Amy's dismal development. Thumb-sucking, nail-biting, blanket-clenching, and bedwetting characterized her infancy and early childhood. She became a hypochondriac and, like Amy, was afraid of the dark and of being left alone. She, too, became lost in role-playing, and the artificial nature of her personality was, if anything, more pronounced than that of Amy's. She had similar problems in school and with her peers. On the surface, she had a far closer relationship with her mother than Amy did with hers, but on psychological tests she gave vent to a longing for maternal affection that was eerily the same as her identical sister's. Beth did seem to be more successful with her friends and less confused than Amy, but she was also less connected to her feelings.

The differences between the girls seemed merely stylistic; despite the differences in their environments, their pathology was fundamentally the same. Did their family lives mean so little? Were they destined to become the people they turned out to be because of some inherent genetic predisposition toward sadness and unreality? And what would psychologists have made of either girl if they had not known that she was a twin? Wouldn't they have blamed the symptoms of her neurosis on the parenting styles of the family she grew up in? What does that say about the presumptions of psychology?

Twins pose questions we might not think to ask if we lived in a world without them. They are both an unsettling presence, because they undermine our sense of individual uniqueness, and a score-settling presence, because their mere existence allows us to test certain ideas about how we are the way we are. Every culture has had to confront the twin phenomenon and come to its own response. Often that response has been to kill the children and to ostracize or kill the mother as well—an implicit acknowledgment of the threat twins can pose to the presumptions of an established order. From ancient times men have been known to cut off one of their testicles in the mistaken belief that it would eliminate the possibility of twin conceptions. Other cultures worship twins as a divine gift; for instance, the voodoo practitioners of West Africa and Haiti exalt twins as supernatural beings with a single soul, who are to be revered and feared. Once a year anyone connected to twins, living or dead, is obligated to make offerings at a ceremonial feast in their honor to avoid "chastisement." In our own culture, we tend to dote on twins and mythologize their specialness through daytime talk shows, which turn them into freaks but which also, to be fair, provide a forum to marvel at the wonder and the mystery of the twin event. Perhaps all these responses are ways of holding twins at bay, since too close a study of twinship might lead to discoveries about ourselves that we are unwilling to make.

In the mid-sixties, when Neubauer began his enquiry into the lives of separated twins, there were no major U.S. twin registries; now the University of Minnesota keeps track of more than 8,000 twin pairs; Virginia Commonwealth University operates the "Virginia 30,000," which follows 15,000 twin pairs plus their siblings, spouses, and parents; there are major registries in Kansas, California, and Kentucky, and smaller ones all over the country. The Veterans Administration maintains records of all twins who served in the Second World War and Vietnam. Pennsylvania State University, with several other institutions, oversees the Black Elderly Twin Study, which uses Medicare records to track down black twins throughout the United States. It is the only large-scale ethnic study in the country, but it may also become the largest study of genetics and aging among women in the world. In Holland, Denmark, Sweden, Norway, Finland, and Australia nearly every twin in the country has been identified. Moreover, in recent years, the technical analysis of twin studies has become increasingly sophisticated and subtle, often taking into account multiple environmental factors, non-twin relatives, and long-term observations. As a result of the variety and complexity of twin studies, along with powerful tools for analysis, the field of behavioral genetics has caused a revolution in the universities that has spilled into political life, reshaping the way our society views human nature and changing the terms of the debate about what government can and should do to improve the lives of its citizens.

Much of the argument over individual differences in intelligence, for instance, arises from the variation between IQ test scores of identical and fraternal twins, the difference being a measure of how much of what we call intelligence is inherited. The field of psychology has been shaken by separated-twin studies, such as the one of Amy and Beth, suggesting that the development of an individual's personality is guided by his genes, with little regard for the family in which he is raised. Matters that instinctively seem to be a reflection of one's personal experience, such as political orientation or the degree of religious commitment, have been shown by various twin studies to be partly under genetic control. Because of the growth of twin studies, and also adoption studies, which examine unrelated individuals reared together (and which complement the study of twins reared apart), the field of behavioral genetics has been able to study traits such as criminality, alcoholism, smoking, homosexuality, marriage and divorce, job satisfaction, hobbies, fears; the results suggest that there are significant genetic contributions in all cases. Even disciplines such as linguistics and economics have seized upon twins as a way of understanding language formation (by looking at twins who create a private idiom), or of calculating the additional earning potential of higher education (by comparing twins who go to college versus twins who don't). There is an air of irrefutability about such studies that make them so appealing. When Linus Pauling proposed that vitamin C could cure the common cold, for instance, twin pairs were separated into two groups, one of which received vitamin C and the other a placebo. Both caught colds, which effectively destroyed Pauling's theory. There are now so many scientists seeking to study twins that the annual festival of twins in Twinsburg, Ohio, allows researchers to set up carnival tents, where browsing twins can stop to take stress tests or fill out questionnaires about their sex lives. Festival organizers even sponsor a prize for the best research project. Last year 90,000 people—most of them twins—attended the event.

All this comes after several decades of heightened political struggle between those, on the one hand, who believe that people are largely the same and that differences are imposed upon them by their environment, and those, on the other hand, who conclude that people differ mainly because of their genes, and that the environments they find themselves in are largely of their own making or choosing. Obviously, the roots of liberal versus conservative views are buried in such presumptions about human nature.

This argument has been raging for centuries, with science entering evidence on either side and public opinion shifting in response. Using twins, and also data derived from adoption studies, scientists can now estimate what proportion of the variation in our intelligence, our personality, our behavior, and even seemingly random life events such as bankruptcy or the death of a spouse, might be caused by inherited tendencies. The broad movement from environmentalism to genetic determinism that has occurred in psychology over the last thirty years has foreshadowed the increasingly popular belief that people are genetically programmed to become the way they are, and therefore little can be done, in the way of changing the environment, that will make an appreciable difference in improving test scores or lowering crime rates or reducing poverty, to name several conspicuous examples.

The hallmark of liberalism is that changes in the social environment produce corresponding changes in human development. But if people's destinies are written in their genes, why waste money on social programs? Such thinking has led to a profound conservative shift in the last thirty years. This can be demonstrated by comparing the shifting climate of opinion in the United States, which in 1965 produced the Great Society—a vast number of social programs designed to improve the health and welfare of the poor, the elderly, and the minority populations—and in 1995 brought about the Contract with America, which generated cutbacks in many of those same programs and marked a change in attitude about what government can be expected to do for its citizens. These changes have taken place not only in the West but in many other countries as well. Indeed, the widespread retreat of communism as a force in world politics is doubtlessly linked to the collapse of faith in social engineering, caused by the failure of communism to create the positive changes expected of it.

The genetic idea has had a tumultuous passage through the twentieth century, but the prevailing view of human nature at the end of the century resembles in many ways the view we had at the beginning. That is that people are largely responsible for their station in life, and that circumstances do not so much dictate the outcome of a person's life as they reflect the inner nature of the person living it. Twins have been used to prove a point, and the point is that we don't become. We are.

2

THE NATURE-NURTURE WARS

TWINS HAVE BEEN confounding humanity from the earliest times, almost as if they were a divine prank designed to undermine our sense of individuality and specialness in the world. Despite the burst of twin scholarship in recent years, they continue to confound science. One reason is that nature offers few experimental models for researchers to compare. Most animals produce litters of polyzygotic—that is fraternal, or non-identical—siblings, who may be of opposite sexes and are thought to be no more alike than ordinary brothers and sisters. The nine-banded armadillo is unique in its ability to produce regular litters of monozygotic—that is, identical—embryos, usually quadruplets. Humans, however, produce both dizygotic (DZ) and monozygotic (MZ) twins.

How and why twins occur is still a mystery; perhaps, as many scientists believe, it is a sort of marvelous birth defect. In any case, identical twins occur in about 3.5 of each 1,000 births, a figure that is both random and universal. Fraternal, or dizygotic, twins are caused by the fertilization of two separate eggs, an event that may take place at different times (and occasionally by different fathers). Theoretically, DZ twins are no more alike than ordinary siblings. MZ twins are thought to result from the splitting of a single fertilized egg, or zygote. It is a form of asexual reproduction. MZ twins have identical genes—they are clones—whereas DZ twins share an average of only fifty percent of their genes, thus creating a statistical opportunity that provides a basis of comparison for nearly every human quality.

Twin studies have always excited political reactions. Sir Francis Galton, Charles Darwin's cousin, invented what is called the classic twin method. Galton was an explorer and geographer who spent several years among the tribes of southwest Africa, where he made the first attempts to compare intellectual abilities between black tribesmen and European colonizers. The chart he produced in 1869 to show the distribution of mental ability among Africans and Englishmen anticipates the disparities that have been so much a part of the recent public debate in the United States. Among Galton's other contributions to social science is the word-association test. His study of twins, however, was his most important legacy, upon which the science of behavioral genetics was created. Galton accurately supposed that twins who looked alike had the same genetic makeup, whereas twins who did not strongly resemble each other were no more genetically alike than ordinary brothers and sisters. He reasoned that traits that were more similar for look-alike twins than for twins who did not look alike were inherent.

> Their history affords a means of distinguishing between the effects of tendencies received at birth, or those that were imposed by the circumstances of their after lives; in other words, between the effects of nature and of nurture.

Galton wrote in 1875:

> The twins who closely resembled each other in childhood and early youth, and were reared under not very dissimilar

> conditions, either grow unalike through the development of natural characteristics which had lain dormant at first, or else they continue their lives, keeping time like two watches, hardly to be thrown out of accord except by some physical jar. Nature is far stronger than nurture within the limited range that I have been careful to assign to the latter.

Galton noted the high correspondence among identical twins for such things as toothaches, onset of disease, and time of death. The twins he studied tended to marry less often than the general population, which led him to suppose that they may have been infertile. "The one point in which similarity is rare is handwriting. I cannot account for this," Galton wrote. It was a matter of particular interest to him, since most of his reporting was conducted by correspondence.*

Galton wrote in an age that had been deeply influenced by the environmentalism of John Stuart Mill, who attributed his own amazing intellect to the early training he had received from his father. The reviews of Galton's book *Hereditary Genius: An Inquiry Into Its Laws and Consequence* were scalding.† "My only fear is that my evidence seems to prove too much and may be discredited on that account, as it seems contrary to all experience that nurture should go for so little," Galton wrote, as he anticipated the reaction to his classic twin experiments.

*There is no evidence that twins have lower fertility than the general population. As for handwriting, Galton may have been confounded by the phenomenon of "mirror-image" twins, who write with opposite hands. Identical twins who write with the same hand usually have extremely similar handwriting.

†In some respects, the response to Galton's work is mirrored in the reviews that greeted Richard Herrnstein and Charles Murray's *The Bell Curve* in the United States more than a century later. Many of the same themes, in particular the heritability of intelligence, prompted angry responses to both books.

> But experience is often fallacious in ascribing great effects to trifling circumstances. Many a person has amused himself with throwing bits of a stick into a tiny brook and watching their progression; how they are arrested, first by one chance obstacle, then by another; and again, how their onward course is facilitated by a combination of circumstances. He might ascribe much importance to each of these events, and think how largely the destiny of the stick had been governed by a series of trifling accidents. Nevertheless all the sticks succeed in passing down the current, and in the long run, they travel at nearly the same rate. So it is with life, in respect to the several accidents which seem to have had a great effect on our careers. The one element, that varies in different individuals, but is constant in each of them, is the natural tendency; it corresponds to the current in the stream, and inevitably asserts itself.

Galton's twin studies were used to justify Herbert Spencer's defense of the British class system, just as more recent twin studies have been invoked to demonstrate racial differences in intelligence, income, and criminality. Galton himself believed that hereditary genius, rather than cultural advantage, accounted for the prominence of Britain's most distinguished families. He proposed that the state should parcel out quotas of children based on the abilities of their parents, thus encouraging the more talented strains and weeding out the defectives. The term he coined for this genetic gardening of the human population was "eugenics."

After the turn of the century, the eugenics movement swept over the United States on the coattails of progressivism. Just as Teddy Roosevelt and Woodrow Wilson set out to reform American politics, a number of prominent academics proposed to make a better world through selective breeding. David Starr Jordan, a biologist who was president of Stanford University, headed a committee of the American Breeders' Association in 1906 to "investigate and report on heredity in the human race." Humans, however, are not as malleable as farm animals and laboratory mice; moreover, the usual experimental techniques were out of the question. Science did not begin to exploit the possibilities of the twin method until the development of various measurements of personality and intelligence in the 1920s, and a better appreciation of the difference between identical and fraternal twins. Galton had intuitively guessed the nature of that relationship, but it would be another half-century before the twinning process was satisfactorily explained, if not understood.

In the 1930s the political character of twin studies showed itself in the extreme. Two powerful political movements, communism and fascism, were spreading across the globe, each based on opposing notions of human nature. It is not surprising that twin research had quite different implications for these two competing systems. The Soviets put an abrupt end to the important and extensive research on twins that was being done at the Maxim Gorky Institute in Moscow, because the study of inherited abilities was at war with the Marxian ideal that people are inherently the same and that differences are imposed upon them by their environment. By 1939, Soviet science was in the grip of T. D. Lysenko, who followed the Lamarckian belief that acquired characteristics could be inherited. This theory so strongly accorded with Marxian theories that it overwhelmed the lack of evidence to support it. Some of the leading geneticists in the Soviet Union were eliminated by Stalinist purges, and those who didn't flee were forced to recant. Lysenko saw the need to place science at the service of socialism, which he did by asserting that similar environments would produce similar people. When applied to agriculture, however, Lysenko's theory resulted in massive crop failures. He was finally discredited in 1964, when the economic cost of his theory became unbearable.

In the meantime, the Nazis had seized the lead (from the Americans) in eugenic research. According to Nazi dogma, the science of eugenics would lead to the creation of a super-race, which would rule the world. Count Otmar von Verschuer, at Frankfurt's Institute for Hereditary Biology and Racial Hygiene, undertook a massive inventory of genetic defects in the German population. He was the most famous twin researcher of his era, pioneering anthropological, psychological, and clinical studies of twins that were widely admired. In 1935 Verschuer wrote in the *Journal of the American Medical Association:* "What is absolutely needed is research on families and twins selected at random," so that one could determine hereditary defects as well as "relations between disease, racial types, and miscegenation." History would soon present an appalling opportunity.

One of Verschuer's students was an ambitious young doctor named Josef Mengele. He was apparently an excellent student, who obtained a medical degree and a doctorate in physical anthropology from the University of Munich, graduating with the highest honors. He then became Verschuer's assistant.

Nazis were already seeking cures for typhoid, yellow fever, smallpox, and other killer diseases by infecting inmates at Dachau and Buchenwald. At Auschwitz, the largest of the Nazi death camps, they were experimenting with mass radiation to find the most efficient method of sterilizing large groups of people. Verschuer managed to secure a grant from the German Research

Society for Mengele to study eye color. Verschuer later wrote that he expected his student to perform anthropological examinations and to send blood samples to his laboratory in Berlin, where he had gone on to become the director of the prestigious Kaiser-Wilhelm Institute of Anthropology and Human Heredity and Eugenics. By now Verschuer was concentrating his research almost entirely on twins, who he believed could unlock the secrets of heredity and help create a master race. There was a similar sense of urgency among eugenicists as there was, in other quarters, among physicists who were digging into the mysteries of atomic power.

Mengele was a man of broad learning, as well as a highly decorated soldier and an outstanding medical officer who had performed bravely on the Russian front. A wound had made him unfit for further combat, and he came directly from the front to Auschwitz. He arrived in the spring of 1943, laden with tests and questionnaires that were likely drawn up by Verschuer. He was a charismatic figure who inspired awe, not only among the German guards, few of whom had any war experience, but also among the inmates, whose lives he held so indifferently in his hands. When the trains that were emptying the ghettos of Poland and Hungary arrived at Auschwitz at dawn each morning, bringing 10,000 inmates a day, Mengele was often the first figure the inmates noticed, standing on the ramp in his Nazi uniform with an Iron Cross on his chest and a riding crop in his hand, smelling of cologne and whistling a Strauss waltz. Many remembered the cheerful way he greeted the new arrivals and separated them into lines on the right or the left, leading to immediate death or slavery. He was forever on the lookout for genetic anomalies: dwarfs, hunchbacks, and Jews with what he considered Aryan features. Twins, however, were his obsession. The guards would race through the incoming refugees calling out for twins in various languages. When he spotted a pair of twins, Mengele would push through the crowd, his face so distorted with eagerness that the new arrivals were struck by his expression. His selection criteria were sufficiently loose that several siblings posed as twins, rightly guessing that it might be their salvation, at least temporarily.

The twins were housed in separate barracks next to the crematorium. Mengele divided the twins by gender, although some of the younger opposite-sex twins were allowed to stay together in the girls' barracks. Unlike other members of the camp, the twins were permitted to wear their own clothes and some were allowed to keep their hair. Eventually 3,000 twins would pass through Auschwitz. They were called "Mengele's children," although at least one set of twins were seventy years old. The handsome doctor brought silk dresses for the girl twins and white pantaloons for the boys; he patted and played with them and gave them chocolates and candy; he organized soccer games with twin teams. The twins, for their part, called him Uncle Mengele, or more intimately, Uncle Pepi. "For twins Mengele was everything," one of the survivors told Robert Jay Lifton, author of *The Nazi Doctors.* "Just marvelous . . . a good doctor." Mengele himself told one of his colleagues, "It would be a sin, a crime . . . not to utilize the possibilities that Auschwitz had for twin research. There would never be another chance like it."

One can imagine the scientific temptation to experiment on twins. The classic twin method, as it evolved from Galton's time, requires a careful determination of zygosity, which Mengele could have done using blood types and fingerprints, which are highly similar (though not identical) among MZ twins. One can then compare both physical and psychological traits to determine which ones are more likely to be genetically influenced. In the early part of this century the classic twin method became a favored tool of the eugenics movement, especially in America. The Germans explored a variant of the classic twin method, which was to study the differences between identical pairs; Verschuer was particularly interested in studying diseases that were present in one MZ twin and absent in the other. His techniques formed the foundation for much of modern medical research using twins. He was also the first to adopt rigorous standards for measuring intelligence in twins and to look at different types of intelligence. Related to Verschuer's method is the twin family design, which notes similarities and differences between family members, particularly children of identical twins, who are not only first cousins but biological half-siblings. (Children of two sets of identical twins would be double-first cousins and biological full siblings, since they would have an average of fifty percent of their genes in common.) Obviously identical twins provide an ideal control for experiments on one sibling and not the other. In some measure, each of these methods would have been known to Mengele, and putting aside the circumstances in which he was operating, there would have been much that could have been learned if scientists were allowed to experiment freely on twins without the constraints of human decency.

The twins were invariably naked as Mengele weighed them and made endless physical measurements. He took frequent X-rays and bled the children almost daily, eventually having to take the blood from their necks when the veins in their arms were no longer productive. He seemed to be fascinated with eye and hair color, and he injected various chemicals into twins' eyes to see if he could turn them blue. He transfused blood from one twin to another. He sterilized some female twins and castrated the males, in what seems to have been an attempt to change their sex. Some twins were kept in isolation; on others he performed gruesome surgeries without anesthesia. Some were starved or deliberately exposed to epidemic diseases; he poisoned one pair and recorded how long it took them to die, with the apparent object of determining if there was any difference in their resistance. A pair of opposite-sex twins, one of whom was hunchbacked, were stitched together back to back. The twins believed, with good reason, that these excruciating experiments were keeping them from the ovens; and yet for most their ultimate destination was Mengele's elaborate pathology lab. He personally killed a number of twins with chloroform injections to the heart as they lay on the dissecting tables. He then opened their bodies, scrupulously comparing their organs to one another. His enthusiasm for this research was apparently limitless; he worked late into the night and would even spend Sundays in his office to put his records in order. He seemed to realize that his research opportunity was a limited one, and this knowledge spurred him into feverish, sleepless activity.

Of the approximately 3,000 twins in Auschwitz only 157 survived Mengele's curiosity. We know very little about what he learned or even what he was looking for. Mengele worried that his records would fall into the hands of the Soviet army, and in fact that may have happened. Verschuer, who was in contact with Mengele throughout the war, destroyed all their correspondence. As a party zealot, Mengele probably was seeking to validate the Nazi dogma of the inherited superiority of the

Aryan race; however, his attempts to change the hair and eye color of the Jews and Gypsies at his disposal suggest that he was also trying to engineer genetic mutations that were scientifically absurd (perhaps his own dark coloring was a spur in this pursuit). One of the prison doctors, Miklos Nyiszli, wrote in his account of Auschwitz that Mengele hoped to discover the secret of multiple births in order to repopulate his depleted nation. There was (and still is) an ongoing debate about the causes of twinning, which were of enormous interest to Verschuer and presumably to his protégé. And yet Mengele never systematically examined the parents of twins, nor did he have the time or the focus to conduct breeding experiments, which in any case would have required several generations of healthy twins who were not submitted to the extraordinary biological stresses of the camp. Despite the testimony of Mengele's colleagues, as well as some of the prisoners, that Mengele was a highly competent researcher, one cannot help but be struck by his scientific naïveté, by the sadism of his experiments, and the wantonness and waste of his precious resources—the twins themselves. One can only suppose that the madness of the entire Nazi enterprise was so total that it overwhelmed scientific discipline and crushed ordinary human reason. If his records ever were to be found, they would be unlikely to be of much interest to twin researchers, except as a cautionary example of the perversion of the scientific impulse by political fanaticism.

It is an interesting question to pose, given the Nazi attachment to genetic predeterminism, whether Mengele could have been a good scientist and a decent human being in another political environment. Was he born to be a monster? Or did he simply adapt to a monstrous situation?

One consequence of Nazism was to discredit genetic theories, and twin studies in particular, for a generation. And in proportion to the fall of genetics was the rise of behaviorism. The behavioristic movement began in the lectures of John B. Watson at Columbia University in 1912, and it quickly produced its own tempestuous controversies. "We have been accused of being propagandists, of heralding our conclusions in the public press rather than in the more dignified scientific journals, of writing as though no one else had ever contributed to the field of psychology, of being bolshevists," Watson recalled in 1930. Watson was doing his work in an age that was convinced of the inheritance of talent, ability, and temperament, that believed in families of genius and families of criminality, that accepted racial differences without question. Watson agreed that physical traits, such as hair color or the length of one's fingers, passed through bloodlines, but the hereditary structure was only waiting to be shaped by the environment; and it might be shaped in a million different ways, depending on the training the child experienced. "Give me a dozen healthy infants, well-formed, and my own specified world to bring them up in and I'll guarantee to take any one at random and train him to become any type of specialist I might select—doctor, lawyer, artist, merchant-chief and, yes, even beggar-man and thief regardless of his talents, penchants, tendencies, abilities, vocations, and race of his ancestors," Watson wrote, in one of the most famous boasts in psychology. Of course, the social implications of Watson's work—especially concerning race and class differences—were shattering. If people were merely creatures of their environment, and not of their genes, then society imposed these differences, rather than simply reflecting them. Twentieth-century liberalism was born in the crusades for social reform that were spawned in part by these behaviorist ideals. The parenting guides of Benjamin Spock carried the behaviorist philosophy into the family. Generations of parents assumed responsibility for their children's talents and defects. Charles Fries did the same for education, instilling the ideal of universal equality as a goal of standardized schooling. Psychotherapy and self-help books became entrenched features of American culture. All these defining trends of modern society arose from the behaviorist doctrine that environment created individual differences.

Watson confronted the question of identical twins by drawing from the very slim literature on twins reared apart available to him in the 1920s. He cited three cases in which twins who had been separated in childhood and lived in different environments were later tested and found to differ significantly in certain respects: one set of twins showed a marked difference in motor skills, another set differed in personality, the third in intelligence. "Suppose we were to take individual twins into the laboratory and begin rigidly to condition them from birth to the twentieth year along utterly different lines," Watson remarked. "We might even condition one of the children to grow up without language. Those of us who have spent years in the conditioning of children and animals cannot help but realize that the two end products would be as different as day is from night."

Watson found an enthusiastic disciple in a young man named B. F. Skinner. During the war, while Mengele was trying to torture the secrets of genetic behavior out of his captive twins, Skinner was at the University of Minnesota teaching economics to rats (who could "buy" food with marbles), and training pigeons to pilot missiles, hoping they could be used instead of humans to conduct warfare. Skinner had refined Watson's principles of behavior to a level of considerable sophistication, as his animal experiments proved, and he hoped to extend his experimental insights into what he called a technology of behavior. He believed that all behavior is genetically based, because we are nothing more than the product of natural selection, but he disputed the notion that there are separate genes for altruism or criminality or any other character trait. What our genes do give us, Skinner reasoned, is the capacity to adapt to our environment. People are not innately good or bad; like any other organism they are determined by their environment. He attacked the notion of individual responsibility. It makes little sense, he believed, to hold people to account for their actions. If one wants to change behavior, then design a different environment. Skinner began the movement toward programmed instruction in public schools, which he expected would cut in half the amount of time required to learn a specified body of material, leading some enthusiasts to predict that eleven-year-olds would soon be earning their Ph.D.'s.

Today, few on either side would argue that we are exclusively the creation of nature or the reflection of nurture. The discussion has evolved into a statistical war over percentages: *how much* of our personality or behavior or intelligence or susceptibility to disease is attributable to our genes as compared to environmental factors, such as the family we are born into or the neighborhood we live in or the years of school we attend. The fulcrum upon which one side rises while the other falls is the concept of heritability, which was first defined by the biologist J. L. Lush in 1940. Heritability, he said, is the fraction of the observed variation in a population that is caused by differences in heredity. Lush was working with farm animals, and he had the luxury of doing breeding experiments. It is easy to establish the transmission of traits in plant and animal populations; in fact, it is the basis of selective breeding. In humans, however, matters are more complex. The most common way of measuring heritability in humans is through twin studies. For any trait, the greater the difference in concordance between identical twins and fraternal twins, the greater the heritability. An example is tuberculosis, which is caused by an infectious organism; however, people have differing degrees of susceptibility to the disease. An identical twin has a fifty-six percent chance of getting the disease if his sibling catches it, but a fraternal twin has only a twenty-two percent chance. The impressive difference between these rates demonstrates a genetic factor at work. If a trait is completely heritable—such as blood type or eye color—then it will be one hundred percent concordant in identical twins and about fifty percent in fraternal twins and other siblings.* The heritability correlation would be a perfect 1.0. If all the differences between siblings are environmental, the heritability would be 0.0.

But environmental factors can also affect traits that are genetically transmitted. Height, for instance, is a highly heritable trait, and in well-nourished Western populations most of the variation in stature is an expression of the genes. The heritability for height among white European and North American populations is about 0.90. This does not mean that if a man is six feet tall, seven inches are due to his environment and the remaining ninety percent to his genes. If an individual is ten inches taller than the average for his population,

*Heritability depends also on frequencies within a population. For instance, if nearly everyone in a population has brown eyes, then fraternal twins will be nearly as concordant for this trait as identical twins.

however, one could estimate that one of those inches is probably accounted for by environment and the other nine inches by his genes. Moreover, heritability can vary significantly in different populations, because the genes require a supportive environment in order to be expressed in the first place. A population that exists on a starvation diet would have little variation in height because growth would be arrested; there would be no way of telling who had tall genes and who had short ones. If one group within the population enjoyed an abundant diet while the rest were starving, the variation of height would be largely environmental. Children of Japanese immigrants who are born and raised in North America tend to be taller than their parents but shorter than the North American average, a difference that is attributed to changes in nutrition (more meat in the diet, for example). The North American grandchildren of those immigrants are taller still, which must mean that environmental effects gain an even stronger hold in the second generation.

Nowhere is the argument about heritability more heated or more consequential in its implications than over the question of intelligence. For much of this century, the debate was grounded in the work of Sir Cyril Burt, who was in his lifetime Britain's most honored and acclaimed psychologist. His name has become associated with a bizarre controversy that scandalized the academic world and is still furiously contested more than a quarter of a century after his death in 1971. Burt was a crusty, opinionated, dominating figure, whose political views were slightly left of center, and whose personality was characterized even by his friends as neurotic and occasionally paranoid. He began his career in 1913 as a research psychologist in the London County Council, which put him in the position of being in charge of all mental and scholastic testing for the London school system. Over the next several decades, Burt founded child guidance clinics and a special school for the handicapped; he developed important new tests and surveys; he wrote a series of books that became landmarks in the rather new fields of juvenile delinquency (*The Young Delinquent*) and mental retardation (*The Subnormal Mind* and *The Backward Child*), which established his reputation as one of the world's leading educational psychologists. This was despite the fact that Burt showed little caution in betraying his class prejudices (describing, for instance, a lower-class white delinquent as "a typical slum monkey with the muzzle of a pale-faced chimpanzee").

Early in his tenure, while working with the London schools, Burt began comparing IQ and scholastic achievement scores on twins and other kinship groups, eventually compiling an unrivaled collection of data on heredity and intelligence. In 1966, at the height of his eminence, he published an epochal paper on fifty-three pairs of identical twins who had been reared apart, a surprisingly large sample of such a rare population. He had accumulated the twins over a period of forty-three years. Separated twins are at once an experiment of nature and an experiment of society. Until that time, there had been only three substantial studies in the literature (Neubauer and his colleagues at the Psychoanalytic Institute had just begun their study). In theory, the average differences between MZ twins reared apart and MZ twins reared together should provide an unassailable measure of environmental effects; however, the environments in which the separated twins are reared may be similar in important ways. Burt's study was particularly stunning because he claimed to have analyzed the socioeconomic status of the wide range of households into which the separated twins were adopted and found that there was no correlation at all between them—and yet the IQs of the separated twins were still very similar. No other study had provided such comprehensive data on the relation of intelligence to social class and social mobility. It appeared to clinch the argument that intelligence is an inherited characteristic and that there is little that can be done in the way of tinkering with the environment to change that.

Three years after Burt's separated-twin study, Arthur R. Jensen, a psychologist at the University of California at Berkeley, published a magisterial attack on compensatory education in the *Harvard Educational Review.* "How Much Can We Boost IQ and Scholastic Achievement?" the title inquired. Jensen's essay, which shook the educational establishment and became the subject of discussion on talk shows and in the White House, was partly based on Burt's work, which was then still untarnished by the allegations of fraud that later covered his work with controversy. In his article, Jensen addressed the racial implications of the genetic transmission of intelligence, and the implications were gloomy indeed. Scores on standardized intelligence tests repeatedly demonstrated that the average black IQ lagged one standard deviation (15 IQ points) behind that of whites. Using the twin studies, which showed the heritability of intelligence to be about 0.80, Jensen argued that the effort to improve IQ among blacks by enriching the environment could produce, at best, a marginal gain, since environmental factors could account for only twenty percent of the difference. He concluded that we should abandon traditional methods of classroom instruction that begin with the premise that people are fundamentally alike in their mental capacities in favor of a model based on genetic diversity.

Of course, there is not a single gene for intelligence—presumably many different genes contribute to the trait that such standardized tests measure—but then, there is not a single gene for height, either. "The simple polygenic model for the inheritance of height fits the kinship correlations obtained for intelligence almost as precisely as it does for height," Jensen wrote. And yet, as several of his critics pointed out, the mean height in the United States and Japan has increased considerably in the last two centuries, too rapidly to be accounted for by genetic factors. Couldn't we expect the same of intelligence in an ideal learning environment?

Jensen conceded that there had been some general increase in height, but he proposed that it could be explained by the increased mobility among populations.

> Outbreeding has increased at a steady rate ever since the introduction of the bicycle. For example, sons of parents who were from *different* Swiss villages were taller by approximately 1 inch than the sons of parents from the *same* village. The increase in heterozygosity, of course, eventually "saturates," and the effects level off, as has already occurred in the U.S. That genetic as well as nutritional factors are a major cause of the increase in actual height is further shown in the fact that approximately the same increase has occurred in all social classes in Western countries even though there have been nutritional differences among social classes.

Jensen concluded his argument: "Thus, the slight increase in the population's mean height over the last two centuries—the environmentalists' favorite counterargument to the high heritability of IQ—itself turns out to be largely a genetic phenomenon!"

Obviously, if Jensen's premise were true, his solution—dividing students by lower and higher abilities—would lead to schools that were resegregated along racial lines, this time because of supposed differences in student intelligence, rather than social discrimination. In fact, his argument was immediately enlisted by attorneys in a federal district court in a last-ditch effort to resist the desegregation of the Greensville and Caroline County, Virginia, public schools. The furor that resulted from the article was more personal than scholarly. For many years afterward, Jensen's mere appearance on a college campus would set off near riots.

In 1971, the psychologist Richard J. Herrnstein, confessing that he had been "submerged for twenty years in the depths of environmentalist behaviorism" as a former student of B. F. Skinner and a psychology professor at Harvard, wrote an equally provocative article simply titled "IQ" in the *Atlantic Monthly.* Herrnstein used much of the same material as Jensen (it became the basis for his book *IQ and the Meritocracy* and later *The Bell Curve*). The *New York Times* quoted him as saying that his "conclusions, if true, amounted to a death sentence for the ideal of egalitarianism." Buttressed by Burt's formidable data from twin studies, the hereditarian argument appeared to have climbed out of the Nazi grave to which it had been consigned.

Within a month after Herrnstein's article appeared, he was invited to speak at Princeton University on an unrelated subject ("The visual field of the pigeon"), but he declined to attend when the university could not make what he thought were sufficient guarantees for his safety. In place of his lecture there was a forum on academic freedom. Herrnstein was defended by Leon Kamin, a psychology professor who had known him at Harvard when both were students there. Kamin, however, was a behaviorist who believed that there was no plausible evidence that intelligence was genetically transmitted. Because Herrnstein cited Burt's famous separated-twin study, Kamin decided to read it for himself. Within ten minutes of starting to read Burt, Kamin decided that "it was transparently clear that the guy was a fraud." He noticed, for instance, that Burt had published several studies of separated twins over the years, beginning with twenty-one pairs in 1955, increasing to "over 30" pairs in 1958, and concluding with the fifty-three pairs in 1966. Despite the fact that the sample size more than doubled over the years, the heritability of intelligence for identical twins reared apart remained exactly the same, even to the third decimal point, 0.771. For that matter, so did the heritability for the control group of twins reared together, 0.944. "The data were simply too perfect to be true," said Kamin. The unlikeliness of such astonishing consistencies was immediately apparent to anyone who had worked with statistics. Kamin also pointed out that Burt offered little information about how he collected the data or even such particulars as the age and sex of the children. "It was a fraud linked to policy from the word go," Kamin charged. "The data were cooked in order for him to arrive at the conclusions he wanted." It served to prove, Kamin asserted, that the IQ test itself was nothing more than "an instrument of oppression against the poor."

Kamin's investigation demolished Burt's scholarly reputation. Soon after that, a science reporter for the *Sunday Times,* Oliver Gillie, published a devastating exposé suggesting that two of Burt's associates, Misses Margaret Howard and J. Conway, who had coauthored papers with Burt and had done much of the actual testing of the twins, "never existed, but were the fantasy of an aging professor who became increasingly lonely and deaf." Burt was no longer alive to respond to these charges, and neither Howard nor Conway stepped forward to provide evidence of her reality. Jensen, who was a friend of Burt's, sought to defend the great man's honor, but when he tabulated the data from Burt's various studies, he came to the same conclusion as Kamin. In a 1974 article in *Behavior Genetics,* Jensen decreed that Burt's correlations were "useless for hypothesis testing"—in effect, reading Burt out of the scientific literature. "It is almost as if Burt regarded the actual data as merely an incidental backdrop for the illustration of the theoretical issues in quantitative genetics, which, to him, seemed always to hold center stage," Jensen wrote. It was a gentler way of saying what Kamin had been charging, that the data were cooked to support Burt's political bias and class prejudice. The loss of Burt's data appeared to have a profound effect on the measure of the heritability of IQ. Christopher Jencks of Harvard recalculated the figures and found that without Burt's data, the correlation of heredity to IQ dropped from about eighty percent to sixty percent.

An authorized biography in 1979 by Leslie Hearnshaw, who had held the Chair of Psychology at Liverpool University until his retirement, largely agreed with Burt's detractors; for one thing, Hearnshaw wrote that only one twin has ever come forward to claim that he had been tested by Burt. That briefly seemed to settle the matter. However, Burt's reputation was at least partially resuscitated by two subsequent biographies, one in 1989 by the psychologist Robert B. Johnson of the University of Nottingham and the other in 1991 by the sociologist Ronald Fletcher of Reading University. The authors concluded that while Burt may have been a careless researcher, he was probably not the complete fraud that his detractors described. Moreover, they pointed out that the attack on Burt's reputation by critics holding opposing political views was itself full of careless, prejudicial reporting. Burt's raw data, which would settle much of the argument, had been partially destroyed by a bomb during the London blitz, and what remained of it was burned by his housekeeper after Burt's death, on the advice of one of Burt's bitterest opponents. On the other hand, Professor N. J. Mackintosh, who teaches experimental psychology at the University of Cambridge, re-examined Burt's twin data in 1995 and found substantial reasons to believe the charges of fraud. It is unlikely that this controversy will ever be satisfactorily resolved.

The bitterness of the battle over twin studies has rarely been matched in the history of academic warfare. The question of what twins tell us about human nature has been clouded by deeply held philosophical, political, and religious ideals. It is certainly true that the history of twin research is one of the most appalling chapters in science, having been born in Galton's aristocratic notions of the natural worthiness of the English upper class, taken to its evil extreme by Nazi eugenicists, and too readily used by American scientists to rationalize racial injustice. On the other hand, it is also true that the critics of twin studies have resorted to ad hominem attacks instead of persuasive scientific experiments. In many university libraries, basic twin research has been ransacked, articles have been ripped out of scientific journals, books have been stolen from the shelves. The 1970s especially were marked by a number of disgraceful episodes in which respectable scientists were harassed and besieged by radical students and by their own colleagues, who seemed to be more interested in stopping the research than in learning the truth. Lost, or at best ignored in the hubbub was the sacrifice of the twins themselves to the cause of science. In some exotic cases, the twins were not even aware of their sacrifice until some odd wind of destiny blew through their lives.

3

The Secret Study

In 1961, Claire Kellman and her husband, Richard, made an application to Louise Wise Services in Manhattan to adopt a child. They were turned down. The Kellmans were émigrés of modest means who had fled Europe during the Nazi era and settled in New York. Only two years before, they had adopted a little girl from the same agency. The officials told the Kellmans that they would have to wait until the daughter was at least three before they could receive another baby. "That was in July," Kellman recalls. "Then in October, on Yom Kippur, we got a letter that they had a baby for us. They called us right away for a meeting. It happened so fast my head was spinning. Two months later we took David home." The Kellmans were told that David was already involved in an intensive child-development study, and although continuing in the program was not made a condition of the adoption, it was repeatedly stressed that the officials wanted the study to continue. The Kellmans agreed. Getting a baby was an uncertain business, as they already knew, and Jewish babies were especially scarce. "We were dealing with Louise Wise Services, which was like dealing with God," Mrs. Kellman says. "You knelt down and kissed their feet and said, 'Thank you for this baby.' "

Nearly every month for twelve years the Kellmans went into the city to visit the Child Development Center on West 57th Street, in the offices of the Jewish and Catholic Board of Family Services. Dr. Peter Neubauer was director of the center. David took intelligence tests and batteries of ability inventories. Every step of his development was observed and recorded. The moment that he first rode a bicycle was captured on film, as were many other hours of him playing with toys and talking to psychologists. The Kellmans were also interviewed, as was David's older sister.

David was small—he weighed less than four pounds at birth—and the Kellmans worried that he might be retarded because he was born prematurely. He turned out to be a bright and playful child, as many psychologists, pediatricians, social workers, and testers could attest. "David began talking very early," Mrs. Kellman says, "and I remember him waking up and saying 'I have a brother.' We would all talk about his 'imaginary brother.' We laughed it off."

Nineteen years after David's birth a peculiar coincidence occurred in upstate New York that would turn his life upside down. Robert Shafran, a dark-eyed young man with a square jaw and a riotous mane of curly black hair, enrolled in Sullivan County Community College, planning to study hotel and restaurant management. Soon after Shafran arrived, people he didn't know began saying hello to him and calling him Eddie. "When I told them I wasn't Eddie, somebody who knew Eddie quite well, who knew that he was adopted, asked me when my birthday was and whether or not I'd been adopted," Shafran later recalled. "And when I told him, he told me that he thought perhaps I had a twin brother." Robert

Shafran and Eddie Galland met that very night. They couldn't believe how much they had in common: for instance, they were both wrestlers and they had the same favorite maneuvers, the same record, the same fastest pin. They had watched the same movies and could mimic the same lines. "It was just wild, surreal," says Shafran. "The next thing we knew we were on the front page of every newspaper in the country."

IDENTICAL TWINS UNITED AFTER MORE THAN 19 YEARS read the headlines on 18 September 1980. The reunited twins story is a venerable chestnut in journalism, one of those rare and quirky good-news items that is guaranteed to gain international exposure, along with stories of pets that have tramped across the country to find their masters. Perhaps what is so compelling about the story of reunited twins is the implicit suggestion that it could happen to anyone; babies actually do get lost or separated, and however rare such an event may be, when a person finds his twin it feeds the common fantasy that any one of us might have a clone, a doppelgänger; someone who is not only a human mirror but also an ideal companion; someone who understands me perfectly, almost perfectly, because he is me, almost me. It is not just the sense of identity that excites us but the difference; the fantasy of an identical twin is a projection of ourselves living another life, finding other opportunities, choosing other careers, sleeping with other spouses. An identical twin could experience the world and come back to report about choices we might have made.

But there is a darker and more threatening side to the story, and this may be the real secret of its grip on our imagination. We think we know who we are. We build up internal barriers to the world, and the barriers are our identity. We struggle through experience to build our character. Our task is to make ourselves unique by understanding who we are and what we like and don't like and what we're willing to stand for. We become the people we choose to be; this is the premise of free will. Suppose, then, we meet an Other who is in every outward respect ourself. It is one thing to imagine an Other who has lived a life, been marked by it, and become uniquely different from us. But if through some whimsical accident of fate we arrive at the same place, if we discover that we are fundamentally alike despite our various experiences, isn't there a sense of loss? A loss not only of identity but of purpose? We wonder not only who we are but *why* we are who we are.

One can imagine, then, the feelings that ran through David Kellman's mind when a friend at Queens College handed him the newspaper that day, and in the photograph that accompanied the story were two young men who looked exactly like him. David Kellman was the third piece of a puzzle that had been separated nearly two decades before. That night all three were on the phone with each other, comparing lives, asking each other questions about school and food and sports and women. "It's all the same! It's all the same!" Eddie kept crying.

When the three of them finally got together, they quickly learned that they had something else in common. Each had been adopted from Louise Wise Services. When they were young each of them used to go to the Child Development Center to be studied. Each had a sister who was two years older and who had also been adopted from the same agency. The architecture of the study began to make itself apparent as they talked. They had each been placed in Jewish homes, but of widely differing social classes. Robert Shafran's family lived in affluent Scarsdale; his father was a doctor and his mother was a lawyer. Eddie Galland's family lived in a middle-class suburb in New Hyde Park, Long Island; his father had a master's degree in industrial arts and taught shop in a local high school. David Kellman's parents were high-school graduates who lived in a blue-collar neighborhood in Queens. As they talked, they wondered why they had been separated.

"I've thought about it for quite some time," says Shafran, who is now studying law in New York. (At one time the brothers operated a restaurant in the SoHo district called Triplets, which is now run by David Kellman alone.) "I'm sure it all started with some distinguished psychiatrist and a roomful of people, and the brilliant idea arises of a new way of studying nature versus nurture. 'Okay, we'll separate these kids and watch them grow.' This is nightmarish, Nazi shit."

Dr. Neubauer did not personally counsel the adoption agency to separate twins and triplets—that decision, he says, was made by Viola W. Bernard, the agency's chief psychiatric consultant—but at the time he was in favor of the idea. He also points out that twins were treated no differently from ordinary siblings. "When a girl would have a child and it would be given up for adoption and then she would go away and have another child, it never occurred to anyone to place them together because they may be siblings. So the advice was given to Dr. Bernard to separate them. She acted on the information available at the time—that twinship was a burden."

Dr. Bernard, now quite elderly and nearly blind, is a professor emeritus of psychiatry at the Columbia University Medical School. "We were of the opinion that the placement of twins who were identical in separate homes had advantages for the children," she says. "They would be able to develop more of their own identity rather than a shared one. The inevitable rivalries are more intensive for these kids. I thought that if we had infants who were identical twins who could be placed separately, that it was also an opportunity to make a research contribution." She acknowledged that there is a "mystique" about twins, but she thought it would be destructive to let the adoptive families or, later on, the twins themselves know the truth about their twinship. "In those days we were playing God, but we had to do the best we could."

Bernard says she counseled the birth mother about the liabilities of placing twins together, but if the mother rejected her advice the twins were not separated. After the twins were born, they were placed in a foster home to await placement. Twins quickly develop a powerful attachment to each other, an effect that is called the "twinning reaction." Once the twins had begun reacting to each other, says Bernard, they were not to be separated because that would have been too traumatic.

According to Bernard, there were four sets of identical twins plus the triplets included in Neubauer's study—a total of eleven individuals—plus "three or four other pairs" who were separated but for various reasons not included. One early pair was used as a prototype to establish the research procedures that were used for the final study.

This study was done in the days before DNA testing could definitively establish whether twins were identical or not. Bernard recalls taking a paper bag of placentas to Columbia University so that geneticists could establish zygosity. This was characteristic of the extreme care that Neubauer and his team took from the very beginning with this rare population. Their study was unique because they were able to study the sequence of development as it occurred. "It was a very intensive study, not only from the observation of the twins, but naturally, the different environments, the total assessment of the child's development, and the parental influences," Neubauer says. "We were surprised to see how extraordinary the concordance is among twins." The difference in intelligence, for instance, was "minimal, almost negligible." There was never a phobia that one of the identical twins or triplets developed that was not shared by their genetic partners. The only differences the Neubauer team observed were in the march of development; one twin might lag behind the other, but would eventually catch up. In other respects, "their nature is as close as possible to identity, in different environments." Given that Neubauer has never published the study even though it ended more than a decade ago, it is impossible to assess the data of what may have been the most ideal twin study ever done, however cruel and ill-advised it may seem to the subjects, some of whom may still not know that they have a twin in the world.

"It was pointed out that these twins might meet each other in later life," says Bernard. "Our position was that if it did happen, then I would talk to them. And if one twin found out, then we felt obligated to tell the other." In fact, at least one set of twins Bernard knows about did discover each other. For the others, she's left an explanatory note in their files at the agency, should they ever ask.

After the triplets' reunion, Mrs. Kellman sought out a psychologist she remembered from the study. She asked the woman why she had let the boys grow up unaware of each others' existence. How could she personally have gone from the Shafran house to the Galland house to the Kellmans', sometimes on the same day, carrying such a secret inside her? "As a scientist," the psychologist replied, "how could I resist?"

4

The Minnesota Experience

In 1979 Professor Thomas J. Bouchard Jr. was sitting in his office at the University of Minnesota, where B. F. Skinner did his landmark work on behaviorism, when one of his graduate students came in with a copy of the *Minneapolis Tribune.* "Did you see this fascinating story about these twins who were reared apart? You really ought to study these. You know, you talk about separated twins in your course." Bouchard began to read:

> LIMA, Ohio. James Springer, brought up believing that his identical twin had died at birth, says meeting his brother face-to-face was "the greatest thing that ever happened to me."
>
> Born in August 1939 in Piqua, Ohio, the brothers were adopted by different families when they were only weeks old. They say they don't know what has happened to their biological parents nor why they were put up for adoption.
>
> Originally, both sets of adoptive parents—Jess and Lucille Lewis and Ernest and Sarah Springer—had been told the other twin had died at birth. But Mrs. Lewis learned the truth by accident when she returned to probate court to complete adoption procedures.

> She recalled that when she said she had named her son James Edward, the court official exclaimed, "You can't do that. They named the other little boy James."
>
> As the years passed, Lewis wondered about his brother, but he said he hesitated to try to find him because he was "afraid it might stir up some problems."
>
> Eventually, however, curiosity overcame Lewis . . .

It was odd enough that both of the twins were named Jim, but it was utterly uncanny that each man had married and divorced a woman named Linda, then married a woman named Betty; the names of their firstborn children were James Alan Lewis and James Allen Springer; each had owned a dog named Toy. The article went on to say that both Lewis and Springer enjoyed carpentry and mechanical drawing and had spent family vacations on the same beach in Florida. Both had worked part-time in law enforcement. They were each six feet tall and weighed 180 pounds. The only apparent difference between them was that Lewis wore his hair short and slicked it back, whereas Springer let his grow longer and combed it forward in bangs. Perhaps it was all a series of absurd coincidences amounting to very little; on the other hand, it might be the riddle of existence itself, the mystery of how we become the people we are, bound up in two soft-spoken, rather bemused, thirty-nine-year-old identical twins who shared a taste for Miller Lite beer and chain-smoked Salem cigarettes.

The subject of twins reared apart was familiar to Bouchard, who is a tall, shambling man, with an open, florid face and bright blue eyes under tangled white brows. Since he came to Minnesota in 1969, Bouchard had been teaching a course in individual personality, vocational interests, values, and mental abilities. Twin studies are the very foundation of this branch of psychology. Not every university offers such a course, in part because race, gender, and class differences are closely compared, which arouses passionate debate over whether such differences are genetic or environmental. Bouchard had been picketed by the Students for a Democratic Society, who demanded that he be fired for teaching the "Nazi theories" of Arthur Jensen and Richard Herrnstein.

This was an unexpected twist for Bouchard, who was a charter member of the Free Speech Movement during his own student days at Berkeley and on one occasion had himself been arrested and had spent a day in jail. He never studied with Jensen there, having been trained as an environmentalist, but later, when Jensen's article appeared in the *Harvard Educational Review,* Bouchard became a convert. His own studies about intelligence had drawn him increasingly into the center of controversy, but it turned out that he had an appetite for intellectual combat.

As it happened, he had already been thinking about pursuing research on twins reared apart, but he had no idea how to go about finding them; there had been only nineteen such cases reported in the United States at the time, and seventy-eight in the world (the Neubauer study was still quite secret). Very few of those had been reared by nonbiological relatives after having been separated early in life, and that made Lewis and Springer all the more exceptional; almost perfect, from the point of view of a behavioral scientist who had spent his career trying to tease apart the influence of nature and nurture on the human personality. Bouchard realized the importance of getting to the twins before they had the chance to create a mythology about themselves, or to reinforce mutual habits and thought patterns, which is one of the most distinctive features of the twinning phenomenon. He immediately invited Jim Lewis and Jim Springer to come to the university for tests. Within an hour Bouchard excitedly persuaded university officials to provide some grant money to study the Jim twins, and he vowed to "beg, borrow, or steal, and even use some of my own money if I have to," for the rest of it. "It was just sheer scientific curiosity," Bouchard says now. "I thought we were going to do a single case study of a pair of twins reared apart. We might have a little monograph." Over the next several weeks he dragooned colleagues from various departments to administer a battery of hastily assembled tests. Finally, only a month after their initial meeting, the Jim twins arrived in the Twin Cities, as the Minneapolis–St. Paul metropolis is called.

On the morning they were to begin the tests, Bouchard took the Jim twins to breakfast. It was the first time he had ever really worked with twins. He intended to brief them on the study, but he found himself obsessing over little details about them: the way each twin picked up his knife, for instance, or the way they had bitten their nails. Each twin had a peculiar whorl in his eyebrow, and Bouchard absently started counting the number of hairs in their brows. "You're staring at us," they told him. Bouchard had to excuse himself. He had been staggered by the similarity of their gestures, their voices, and the morphology of their bodies. These men had lived entirely separate lives, and yet if Bouchard closed his eyes he couldn't tell which twin was talking.

"We'd start early in the morning and finish in the evening," Jim Springer recalls about his first trip to Minneapolis. "They'd take Jim [Lewis] one way and I'd go the other. Maybe we'd pass each other in the hallway, that was it." Bouchard had read carefully the criticism of previous twin studies and knew the importance of testing the twins separately, using separate investigators, to keep from contaminating the results with the interviewer's expectations or gossip by the twins. The Jims had grown up less than a hundred miles from each other in western Ohio, so their values and many of their cultural references were similar, and of course any two people are bound to find that they have tastes, habits, experiences, and even friends in common if they live in the same society. In the case of the Jim twins, however, it was more difficult to find differences. According to their life histories and the inventories they filled out, each lived in the only house on his block, with a white bench around a tree in the backyard; each had elaborate workshops where they made miniature picnic tables (Lewis) or miniature rocking chairs (Springer); each followed stock-car racing and hated baseball. Their wives told the Minneapolis researchers that both Jims were romantics who left love notes around the house, but they were also anxious sleepers who ground their teeth at night and bit their nails to the quick during the day.

The Jims had extraordinarily parallel health histories as well: both had identically high blood pressure and had experienced what they thought were heart attacks, although no actual heart disease was diagnosed; both had had vasectomies; both had hemorrhoids; both had "lazy eye" in the same eye. The measurable features of their personalities, such as sociability, flexibility, tolerance, conformity, and self-control, were all so similar that they could have been the same person, as were their mental ability scores. "The only difference is that I would talk about my feelings where Jim felt more comfortable writing about them," says Springer. Bouchard was struck as well by the fact that their speech patterns, their body language, the way they sat in a chair or shook hands, were practically indistinguishable. Certain findings had immediate consequences. For instance, since their teenage years both Jims had suffered the same kinds of migraine headaches, which until then were not thought to have a genetic basis. Also, at one point in their adult lives both Jims put on ten pounds at the same time. Was there some kind of genetic programming at work? Such things had been suspected, but now there was a way of comparing major life changes. The possibilities for the study seemed to open endlessly. Bouchard stopped thinking about doing a little monograph.

"We got quite a bit of publicity," Bouchard recalls. "*People* magazine ran a story. They were on the *Johnny Carson Show.* They really fascinated everybody. And so I wrote a grant proposal. I had no idea it would become a life study." As a result of the publicity, however, other separated twins began to surface, creating a research bonanza. Within a year of the Jims' reunion, Bouchard had studied fifteen other sets of separated twins and put together a team of six psychologists, two psychiatrists, and nine other medical experts.

A routine developed. The twins usually arrive in Minnesota on a Saturday (international visitors arrive on Friday). They have been asked to bring whatever birth certificates, adoption papers, photographs, school and medical records, awards, and letters they can find. Bouchard usually greets them at the airport. Often the spouses or parents come as well, to be included in the family studies that have been added to the program. Sunday afternoon the twins go to Elliott Hall, where one twin begins writing out his life history, while the other twin, in a separate room, takes the first of many personality assessments, which include the Minnesota Multiphasic Personality Inventory, the Myers-Briggs Type

Indicator, and the California Psychological Inventory. When they are finished, they switch places. Monday at eight, the first full day, the twins go to the hospital. Electrodes are attached to their scalps for electrocardiograms; the twins also get a chest X-ray, a hearing test, and endure ninety-nine different physical measurements, including such things as arm size, head length, nose depth, ear shape, the diameter of the eyes. They occupy the rest of the morning by taking tests of mental abilities. After lunch, they have their fingerprints taken and their allergies tested, submit to a complete physical examination, then complete personality assessments until five-thirty. Tuesday, the longest day of the week, begins with a donation of blood before breakfast and again ninety minutes later, in order to measure the rate of insulin production. For the next twenty-four hours the twins wear monitors that record their pulse, blood pressure, and body temperature. They undergo lengthy psychiatric interviews and medical life histories. After dinner, the twins are faced with a sexual history questionnaire that is so intimate that many simply refuse to finish. Wednesday morning is full of visual and dental exams. Thursday, the twins are greeted with more mental abilities tests, voice sampling, psychomotor tasks to measure hand-eye coordination, and the Wechsler Adult Intelligence Scale. Each twin is videotaped lighting a cigarette if he smokes, catching a pair of keys that are tossed to him, drawing pictures of a house and a person, writing a paragraph, and walking across the room and shaking Professor Bouchard's hand; the point is to make a visual record of their physical mannerisms. Friday features information-processing tasks, such as sorting objects into trays, and an interview that explores the major life stresses that each twin has experienced. The afternoon is occupied by a two-hour pulmonary exam and more tests of mental abilities and personality assessments. Saturday concludes with a final round of mental abilities, information processing, psychomotor tasks, and personality inventories.

One can imagine the state the subjects are in when the week finally ends; it wears the staff out as well. But by two o'clock on Saturday Bouchard's team will know as much about the twins as it is possible to measure after approximately fifty hours of tests. They will know what they eat, the books they have read, their sexual orientation and predilections, the television shows they watch, how much their hands quiver when they hold a stick in a hole, their musical tastes and talents, their phobias, their childhood traumas, their pulse rates at rest and under stress, the diameter of their pupils and how quickly they contract in the light, the amount of decay in their teeth, their hobbies, their values, the way they sit in a chair. Many of the twins return for follow-up studies, as do family members. Because of the Minnesota project, separated twins have become one of the most densely studied populations in the history of psychology.

Many memorable characters have passed through Elliott Hall. Among the early pairs were Daphne Goodship and Barbara Herbert, who, like the Jims, had been adopted separately as infants and lived thirty-nine years apart. Barbara had grown up in a modest home in Hammersmith, in London, as the daughter of a city gardener. Daphne had a middle-class childhood north of London in Luton, where her father was a metallurgist. Barbara had learned that she was a twin when she needed a birth certificate to qualify for her pension fund. There she learned that her birth name was Gerda Barbara Jacobson, but she also noticed that the doctor had jotted down the time of her birth, which in Britain is only used as a way of distinguishing between twins. Barbara finally met her identical twin at King's Cross Station in London in May 1980. Each appeared wearing a beige dress and a brown velvet jacket. They greeted each other by holding up their identical crooked little fingers—a small defect that had kept each of them from ever learning to type or play the piano. They discovered that they are both frugal, like the same books, had been Girl Guides, hated math in school, chose blue as their favorite color—the sort of incidental things that many people discover they have in common—but there were other commonalities that were harder to explain. Both had the eccentric habit of pushing up their noses, which they each called "squidging." They liked their coffee black and cold. Both had fallen down the stairs at the age of fifteen and claimed to have weak ankles as a result. At sixteen, each had met at a local dance the man she was going to marry. They each suffered a miscarriage with their first pregnancies, then proceeded to have two boys followed by a girl (although Barbara had two more children after that). Both put on weight easily, although Daphne, the more serious dieter, weighed twenty pounds less than Barbara. And both laughed more than anyone else they knew, which was why Bouchard nicknamed them the Giggle Sisters when they arrived in Minnesota shortly after their first meeting. During the physical examinations, the sisters learned that each had a minor heart murmur and an enlarged thyroid gland. They also had identical brain waves. Although both of the sisters loved to talk, Bouchard was interested in the fact that each fell silent whenever the conversation turned to more provocative subjects, such as politics. In fact, neither had ever voted, except once, when they were both employed as polling clerks. Avoidance of controversy was supposed to be classic learned behavior; was it possible that it had a genetic component as well? And if so, how?

There were two male pairs with gay members. In one, neither member of the pair knew of the other's existence until one of them went into a gay bar in a neighboring town and was mistaken for his brother. They had very similar histories. Both had been hyperactive as children and had learning disabilities; both were highly emotional and subject to depression; and both had been actively gay since the age of thirteen. After their reunion, they actually became lovers.* In the second pair one twin was exclusively homosexual and the other considered himself exclusively heterosexual, despite an affair with an older man when he was a teenager. Among the separated twins who came to Minnesota there were also four lesbian twin sets with one member who was gay or bisexual, but in every case the other twin was straight.

Many of the twin pairs had similar fears. A British pair of sisters feared ocean bathing and would get into the water only by backing in slowly. Another pair of sisters arrived in Minneapolis each wearing seven rings on her fingers. One pair reported having had similar nightmares, imagining doorknobs and fishhooks in their mouths and smothering to death. Few twins were such pure specimens as the Jims, whom Bouchard labeled "the most valuable pair that has ever been studied." Usually the pairs had been separated later in their childhood, or had been reunited years before, or had been raised by other relatives. Oddly enough, the degree of similarity between them did not seem to be positively correlated with their age at separation; those twins, like the Jims, who had been separated early tended to be even more similar than those who had been separated later.

*Gay twins who have been reared together typically deny any feelings of sexual attraction for each other. This seems to be characteristic of siblings who have been raised together.

Again and again Bouchard and his team would be flabbergasted by the similarities, the unheard-of coincidences, and the counterintuitive findings that their tests would turn up. "We were not ready for what we found," he reported after a year of study. "Worse yet, we do not feel we have adequately captured the phenomenon. Many differences between the twins are variations on a theme more than anything else."

Jack Yufe and Oskar Stöhr were born in Trinidad in 1933 and were split apart a few months later in a bitter divorce, brought on by the father's violent behavior. Jack stayed in Trinidad with their father, a Jewish merchant in Port of Spain. Oskar went to live in the all-female household of their German maternal grandmother, who was Catholic. She was also a devoted Nazi. While Oskar was preparing to become a member of the Hitler Youth, Jack was exploring his Jewish identity. At the age of sixteen, he was sent to Israel to work in a kibbutz. He later served in the Israeli navy. In 1954, he decided to emigrate to the United States, and stopped off in Munich to meet his brother for the first time since their separation twenty-one years before. It was hard for them to communicate, because Oskar spoke only German, whereas polyglot Jack spoke English, Spanish, some Yiddish and Hebrew—but not German. Jack was shocked when the translator advised him not to mention he was Jewish because Oskar's stepfather still didn't know there were Jews in the family. The reunion was chilly and brief. Jack moved to San Diego, where he opened a clothing and appliance store. Oskar stayed in Germany, where he became a factory supervisor. Twenty-five years passed, with little more communication than a Hanukkah card from the Yufes each year and a Christmas card in reply from Oskar's wife. One day in 1980 Jack's wife read about the Jim twins and the

Minnesota studies, and Jack decided that it might be a good idea to meet his twin again, this time on neutral ground. He contacted Bouchard, who eagerly agreed to fly them both to Minneapolis to become the eleventh pair to be studied.

One of the objections to twin studies is that the twins are often reared in similar environments that might account just as well as genes do for the often startling similarities of these Minneapolis encounters. Also, say the critics, twins are prone to mythologize their similarities in a bid for publicity, movie, and book deals, or at the least, a consoling sense of specialness after being partly robbed of their identity. If environment was ever going to assert itself in these studies, Oskar and Jack should have been an ideal pair. The contrasts in their upbringings, their cultures, their family lives, were overwhelming. Moreover, they didn't seem to like each other enough to create the kinds of identity legends that the critics suspected were at the bottom of the separated-twin sagas.

Bouchard was standing with Jack at the Minneapolis airport when Oskar came off the plane. "I remember Jack pulling in his breath because Oskar walked exactly the same way he did," Bouchard recalls. "They have a kind of swagger to their body." Each sported rectangular wire-rimmed glasses, a short clipped moustache, and a blue, two-pocket shirt with epaulets. They shook hands but did not embrace. Soon they were sitting in Elliott Hall in separate rooms, answering some 15,000 questions about themselves.

As it turned out, Jack and Oskar had dozens of quirky habits in common, such as storing rubber bands on their wrists, reading magazines from back to front, flushing the toilet before using it, and dipping buttered toast in their coffee. They also shared a taste for spicy foods and sweet liqueurs. They differed in certain obvious respects: Oskar, for instance, was married, while Jack was divorced, but Jack noticed that Oskar expected his wife to take care of all needs without question, much as Jack himself had done when he was married. Jack regarded himself as a liberal Californian, and he saw his brother as "very traditionalistic, typically German." Oskar was a skier, Jack was a sailor. Oskar was a devoted union man, Jack a self-employed entrepreneur. Of course they had lived profoundly different lives, so that their memories, their experiences, their religious and political orientations—in other words, the interior world, the raw stuff of selfhood—were unique. Their personality profiles were strikingly similar, however, despite the fact that they had been raised in such opposing cultures. Bouchard observed that their tempos, their temperaments, their characteristic mannerisms—their style of being in the world—were far more alike than different, similarities that were all the more surprising because Oskar was raised entirely by women and Jack had grown up with his father.

One night in Minneapolis, the two men went to see a hypnotist in a cabaret. As the hypnotist was attempting to put a volunteer into a trance, and was dramatically counting backward, Oskar abruptly sneezed—loudly, so that everyone in the club was startled. "He does that all the time," Oskar's wife whispered to Jack, who was astonished. One of his favorite pranks was to step into a crowded elevator and let out a loud fake sneeze just to watch everybody jump.

The team studying these twin pairs was at a loss to explain how these uncanny coincidences might have happened. Was it possible that people could be wired in such a way that they were programmed to marry people named Betty and Linda, or squidge their noses, or sneeze on elevators? Did these events have meaning or were they just random, freak happenstances? Clairvoyance is a part of twin lore; twins frequently report that they experience sharp pain when one is injured, or that they know when the other is about to call; some have even reported being able to see out of the other twin's eyes when they are experiencing some dramatic event. These suggestive psychic connections between identical twins could explain some of the mysterious synchronicities, but they have been rarely tested and never confirmed. Moreover, many of the twins had not been aware that they had a genetic companion in the world.

Bouchard throws up his hands when he talks about the coincidences. "We had a lot of discussions about how you could do anything with that information, and it turns out it would be a massive, massive job. It's a big world with lots of possibilities. For example, take the names of the kids." He was referring to the fact that several twins who had been raised apart gave their children identical or highly similar names. "We know names are not randomly distributed. They come in waves. They reflect popular taste. When Jack Kennedy was president, there were a lot of kids named Jack. We know that these are nonrandom events. And so the probability that two people have the same name can't be validated against some random action. What you need is a population of couples the same age as the twin couples with their kids, and then you'd need to know the frequencies of all these names. Think about how much work you'd have to do to gather that kind of information—but then you'd have to do it for everything! About the car they owned! About the beach they went to! What they named their dog! You'd have to collect that data from every pair. And then, what would it tell you?"

Those early sets of twins—the Jims, the Giggle Sisters, the Nazi and the Jew—created a sensation not only in the popular press but in scientific journals as well.

Money, which had been so hard to capture in the early years of the Minnesota study, soon came along in the form of government funds and grants from private foundations that had an interest in twin research. Foremost among the foundations backing Bouchard's research is the Pioneer Fund, a New York foundation that has roots in the eugenics movement of the thirties and that has had a history of backing projects that advocate racial separatism. The Pioneer Fund has given the Minnesota project over $1.3 million, more than any other project in the fund's history. In the sixteen years since Bouchard met the Jim twins, his study of reared-apart twins has included 132 individuals who are identical twins; two sets of identical triplets; another two sets of mixed triplets (a pair of identical twins plus a fraternal third member); seventy-six individuals who are same-sex fraternal twins and twenty-six who are opposite-sex fraternals; plus more than a hundred other people who are spouses, friends, adoptive parents, and siblings of reared-apart twins. The youngest set of twins was eleven, the oldest seventy-nine. The center also maintains a substantial registry of reared-together twins, helps separated twins find their siblings, and provides information of interest to twins over its own toll-free telephone line (800-IMA-TWIN) for its still ongoing study.

At first, many of the findings seemed quirky, at odds with one's expectations of how personalities are shaped. Religious attachment, for instance, would seem to be largely a creation of the family environment. Even some very distinguished behavioral psychologists believed that religiosity had no genetic basis. However, when the Minnesota team studied religious interests, attitudes, and behaviors of twins reared apart, as well as twins reared together, they found that genetic factors accounted for about fifty percent. Religious affiliation, on the other hand—one's denomination or belief—was largely environmental. As Bouchard and others extended their studies of personality, a pattern emerged: characteristically, about half of the variance in most measurable personality traits turned out to be genetic. For the commonly tested traits of extroversion, agreeableness, conscientiousness, neuroticism, and openness, Bouchard found the overall heritability to be 0.41. Other researchers found that the heritability of radicalism and tough-mindedness was 0.65 and 0.54; for authoritarianism the heritability estimate was 0.62. Genetic influences on occupational interests, on the other hand, were slightly less heritable.

Of all the twin pairs that have come to the university, there were only two "dog people"—one showed her dogs and the other taught obedience classes—and they were a reared-apart twin pair. Only two of the more than 200 individual twins who had been reared apart were afraid to enter the soundproof chamber in the psychophysiology lab unless the door was left open — again, an MZ pair, the same women who insisted on entering the ocean backward. There were the two men who independently offered a correct diagnosis of a faulty bearing on Bouchard's car, two fashion designers, two captains of volunteer fire departments, two who had been married five times—in each case, a pair of reared-apart identical twins.

One of the Minnesota researchers, David Lykken, tried to test the hypothesis that identical twins were sending telepathic communications to each other, which might explain some of the startling coincidences. He placed a pair of female identicals in separate sleeping chambers and monitored their brain waves through the night. At intervals, one twin would hear a recording of her sister's voice calling out her name—"Mary! Mary! Mary!"—two or three times. The twin in the other lab, at different times, would hear her sister calling out "Sue! Sue! Sue!" Lykken's notion was that telepathy might work better during sleep. Mary's brain waves would indicate that she heard Sue calling her; perhaps then she would respond by sending out some kind of mental signal that would register with Sue. The first pair of twins actually did seem to communicate as Lykken had predicted, but then he discovered an error in the computer program that made the effect seem far less significant. A British researcher on paranormal psychology, Susan Blackmore, found that twins who were placed in separate rooms and asked to draw whatever came to mind would often draw similar things, but if they were asked to draw a picture and psychically transmit it to the other twin, there was little evidence of telepathy. The conclusion that Blackmore drew was that while twins may seem clairvoyant, it is only because they are thinking the same thing—a remarkable effect, but not the one she was studying.

Obviously, extrasensory perception would be a useful quality for espionage, so it is not surprising that the U.S. Central Intelligence Agency has performed experiments to determine whether twins have a significant ability to transmit knowledge telepathically. Twin lore is replete with anecdotes suggesting that illness or trauma in one of a pair of identical twins could be sensed by the other twin, even when they are far apart and unaware of the other's status. The unnamed CIA experimenters noticed that the brain's alpha rhythms can be elicited simply by closing one's eyes in a lighted room. They placed identical twins in separate rooms twenty feet apart and told them to open or close their eyes only on demand. Their brain patterns were carefully monitored. The experimenters theorized that eye closure in one twin should trigger alpha rhythms in both. Out of thirteen sets of twins, two sets produced the results that the CIA was looking for. None of the unrelated subjects involved as controls in the test showed any telepathic connection. "Extrasensory induction of brain waves exists between individuals when they are completely separated. It certainly is not a universal trait in all identical twins," the experimenters concluded. "Because of the paucity of controlled data, contrasted with the voluminous pseudoscientific and highly emotional information available in the realm of extrasensory perception, it appears unwise to draw any conclusions or to make any statements regarding these aspects of the current investigations." This provocative finding suggests that there is at least some basis for believing the stories twins so often tell about their telepathic awareness of each other when they are apart.

Twins also share genetic traits that do not run in families: they are idiosyncratic features that seem to be exclusive to identical twins. "Behavior geneticists have been talking for years about polygenic traits, like stature and IQ, that are determined by multiple genes in different locations on the genome, working together in an additive way," Lykken says. "But some traits may be determined by *configurations* of genes. For example, musical talent runs in families but singing ability does not." A singer requires talent, proper vocal apparatus, a musical ear, and perhaps certain features of personality that would encourage public displays. Each of these traits is partly genetically determined, which is why identical twins have such remarkably similar voices, but ordinary siblings seldom have voices that are really alike. Beauty, Lykken proposes, is another example of the configuration of various genetic traits that are not remarkable by themselves; traits of leadership and scientific genius may be as well. Perhaps the idiosyncrasies, the weird coincidences, and the similarity of life events can be explained by the fact that identical twins are not just the sum of their individual genes but the product of many genetic constellations, which in a powerful, synergistic manner determine behavior, mannerisms, tics, social attitudes, marital relations, clothing choices, and political affiliations. Identical twins, in some respects, can be even more alike than we knew.

The mountain of data compiled by the Minnesota team, along with ongoing twins research in Boulder, Stockholm, and Helsinki, stunningly tipped the balance in the nature-versus-nurture debate. Bouchard and his collaborators assessed a variety of personality characteristics, such as a sense of well-being, social dominance, alienation, aggression, and achievement, which they described in an important article in the 1988 *Journal of Personality and Social Psychology.* On the question of IQ, the Minnesota team found a higher correlation for separated MZ twins than most previous twin studies: 0.76, almost exactly the figure that Cyril Burt stood accused of fabricating. Identical twins reared together score 0.86, as much alike as the same person tested twice (0.87). In the personality domain, the Minnesota team attributed about half of the measurable variation to genetic causes. (These studies measure statistical differences within populations. They do not imply that fifty percent of any one individual's personality is genetically acquired.)

Bouchard's team compared the personality scores for separated MZ twins and separated DZ twins against the scores for twins of both types who had been reared together. They concluded that identicals reared apart were about as much alike as—in some cases *more* alike than—identicals reared together. Moreover, there was not a single one of those personality traits in which fraternal twins reared together were more alike than identicals reared apart. How could this be? Wouldn't twins who had grown up in the same family, gone to the same schools and churches, and been exposed to the same values and traditions have been similarly shaped by those influences? If, as the Minnesota team was claiming, half of the variance in personality in a population was genetic in origin and the other half was environmental, why wouldn't fraternal twins reared together be far more alike in their personalities than identicals reared apart?

The answer to this paradox had been suggested before, but not with the force of so much data. "None of the environmental variance is due to sharing a common family environment," the Minnesota team asserted. *None?* Bouchard and his colleagues repeated the charge in an unsettling 1990 article in *Science.* "The effect of being reared in the same home is negligible for many psychological traits," the Minnesota team wrote. Even in social attitudes, such as religiosity and traditionalism, adult identical twins were about as much alike regardless of whether they had been reared together or apart. "We infer," the Minnesotans wrote, "that the diverse cultural agents of our society, in particular most parents, are less effective in imprinting their distinctive stamp on the children developing within their spheres of influence—or are less inclined to do so—than has been supposed."

Bouchard's findings confirmed a startling, much-debated adoption study that had been done at the University of Minnesota a few years before his twin studies began. Sandra Scarr and Richard A. Weinberg compared the IQs of adopted children with those of their adopted parents and their biological parents. As is typical in adoption studies, the IQs of the children were higher than those of their biological parents, but still strongly correlated. The inference usually drawn from this information is that the adopted parents tend to be of a higher intelligence and a higher social class than the parents who surrender their children for adoption, and that the improved scores reflect this enriched environment. Scarr and Weinberg pointed out, however, that the children's IQ did not correlate at all with the IQ or the social class of their adoptive parents. They concluded that most families provide "functionally equivalent" environments; in other words, a person could grow up in one family as well as another and still have, at the end of adolescence, the same IQ in either case. Scarr and Weinberg qualified their observations to point out that they were not talking about extremes of environment; children raised in truly deprived circumstances would no doubt show the effects. But the elevation in IQ that was supposed to follow the rise in economic status simply wasn't present. "Why are the relatively poor families rearing adopted children whose IQ scores are nearly as high as those in professional families?" they asked. "It must be that all of these seeming environmental differences that predict so well the outcome differences among biological children are not primarily *environmental* differences, but indices of genetic differences among the parents and their biological offspring." In other words, the lower intelligence of the lower working class was a result of their genes, not their situation. It was the same observation made by Francis Galton a century before.

Bouchard's studies began at a time when twin research was struggling to regain scientific respectability; now twin studies dominate much of the research in personality. Autism, for instance, was believed by the behaviorists to have been caused by "refrigerator mothers" who raised their children without enough affection; similarly, schizophrenia was supposed to have been generated by mothers who repeatedly placed their children in emotional binds. Down syndrome was said to be the result of physical and psychological traumas the mother may have suffered during pregnancy. The guilt felt by parents who stood accused of damaging their children is easy to imagine. Twin studies have now established a strong genetic component to many forms of mental illness, including not only autism and schizophrenia (Down syndrome has been shown to be a chromosomal anomaly), but also phobias and neuroses, which were previously presumed to be caused almost exclusively by traumatic emotional events. The Minnesota studies attribute forty-six percent of the personality variables they have measured to genetic factors, and practically none to family environment. Many physical ills, from acne to heart disease, are highly heritable, and even infectious diseases, such as German measles and chickenpox, appear to have a genetic basis, probably because of an inherited vulnerability in the immune system. On the other hand, twin studies have demonstrated that respiratory diseases and many cancers are largely environmental in origin.

Even more controversial and confounding have been twin studies of behavior. A Virginia study of 1,000 female twin pairs concluded that genetic factors account for about half the risk of developing problems with alcohol. Behaviors as diverse as smoking, insomnia, choice of careers or hobbies, use of contraceptives, consumption of coffee (but not, oddly enough, consumption of tea), menstrual symptoms, and suicide have all been shown to have far higher rates of concordance for identical than for fraternal twins, suggesting that they are more influenced by genes than previously suspected. German studies during the Nazi era implicated criminality as a heritable trait (this finding was used to justify the widespread sterilization practices during that period), but the reared-apart studies have shown little evidence to support the thesis that criminality is genetic and much to suggest that the environment is largely to blame.*

A 1986 survey of Australian twins posed fifty questions about social attitudes and found a significant genetic component for forty-seven of them, including such diverse items as socialism, the authority of the church, the death penalty, chastity, and birth control. Only three motley subjects—coeducation, the use of straitjackets, and pajama parties—showed no meaningful genetic influence. This seemed particularly strange because one would expect the family environment to play an almost overwhelming role in determining social attitudes; and yet, that simply wasn't found. An especially interesting Swedish study of elderly twins, led by Gerald E. McClearn, a behavioral geneticist at Pennsylvania State University, looked at life events such as retirement, the death of a child, the mental illness of a spouse, and financial reverses, many of which might seem, almost by definition, to be accidents of the environment. The researchers concluded that forty percent of the variance of their total life-events score was attributable to genetic effects. Adding to the puzzle was that fact that twins who had been reared apart were somewhat more alike in terms of their major life events than twins who had been reared together.

Underlying these momentous assertions is an insistent unanswered question: how? Is there a gene for

*According to a 1995 study by M. J. Lyons et al., the heritability of antisocial behavior has been shown to increase from 0.07 in adolescence to 0.43 in adulthood, while the contribution of environmental effects decreases from 0.31 to 0.05 during the same period of time—a complete turnaround. On the other hand, a more recent study of more than 2,500 Australian twins found a heritability correlation for adolescent misconduct of 0.71 and no environmental effect. It seems this issue is very much unresolved.

neurosis or alpine skiing or traditional values? Nothing in molecular biology indicates anything of the sort. The assumption of the twin model is that if one controls for the genes, by comparing identical versus fraternal twins, then the differences must be environmental; and further, if one controls for the environment, by comparing reared-apart identicals to reared-together identicals, then what is the same must be genetic. The logic seems to be unassailable, but it leads to unanswerable riddles. "Events have no DNA," the authors of the Swedish study conceded; "therefore, genetic factors cannot affect events per se. However, life events are defined as events that happen to people—their experiences. Genetic influence on experiences must be due to genetically influenced characteristics of individuals, not of the environments."

5

THE CRITICS RESPOND

IN THE EARLY 1950S, James Shields, a British researcher, went on BBC television and made a public appeal for separated twins to step forward to be tested. More than forty separated sets of identical and fraternal twins responded. These were, of course, twins who knew of their kinship. Shields concluded in his own account of the project that family environments can vary significantly without affecting the profound similarity of separated identical twin pairs; on the other hand, identical twins brought up together can vary quite widely. Unlike the Minnesota team, Shields provided the raw data in the form of case studies of each of his twins, and it was clear that many of the so-called "separated twins" Shields studied had been raised by branches of the same family and had been companions during childhood.

Leon Kamin, the psychologist who led the attack on Burt, has become perhaps the most outspoken critic of twin studies. He charges that most separated identical twins haven't really been apart anywhere near the amount of time that Bouchard and his colleagues have advertised, and if they had, presumably they would be far less similar than they seem to be. For instance, when Kamin examined the twins cited in Shields's sample, he found that the IQ correlation for those who had been brought up in related families was 0.83, while for those brought up in unrelated families it was 0.51. Shields himself, however, recalculated his own data based on the similarity of environments. His correlation for twins who grew up in the most similar environments was 0.87—about the same as Kamin's figure—but for twins who grew up in the least similar environments the correlation was 0.84. Environmental differences, in other words, essentially made no difference in the intelligence of identical twins.

Twins have been separated for a variety of reasons, such as financial hardship, the death of the mother, and illegitimacy. Sometimes twins were divided among family members; in those cases, it was usually the maternal grandmother who received one of the twins and the birth mother who kept the other. In one case that Shields studied, the biological father, a bankrupt Scandinavian ship's carpenter, sold one of his twins to a wealthy South American doctor to settle his debts. Given the oddity of their circumstances, it's difficult to know to what extent separated twins represent the general population. And despite the intensive research and interest in identical twins reared apart, fewer than 300 pairs have been identified, so the entire sample remains small.*

But in any case, if the environment shapes intelligence, then presumably the age of separation of the twins, and the amount of time that they spent together during their formative years, would be critical factors. "Bouchard reports that there is no correlation between

*There may be many more to be discovered in Japan. According to Professor Juko Ando, a twins researcher in the Department of Education of Keio University, twins born in rural areas were often separated because of the stigma attached to multiple births. This practice has died out in recent decades.

the age of separation and the similarity of IQ, but I can't do the analysis," Kamin complains. "Nit-picking critics like me don't have the opportunity to go over their data." The Minnesota team no longer publishes case studies as it did in the early days of the program, and Bouchard refuses to release raw research material, citing privacy concerns on the part of the twins. "I wouldn't let Leon Kamin anywhere near it," he says. "If he has a legitimate question, we could answer it."

Susan Farber, a clinical psychologist now in private practice in Boise, Idaho, reviewed all known case studies of separated twins (excluding the Burt data) in her 1981 book, *Identical Twins Reared Apart,* and found only three examples out of 121 cases cited worldwide in which the twins truly were separated shortly after birth, reunited as adults with no intervening contact, and studied at their first reunion. (Farber did not deal with the Minnesota project, which was only getting started when her book appeared, nor was she aware of the Neubauer study. According to Bouchard, the average age of the twins who have come to Minnesota is forty; they have spent thirty years apart, so they have had a decade or so of contact before he has a chance to test them. In several instances, however, he has personally reunited twins who have never met before. The average age of the twins at the time of separation was five months.) Farber's survey left her unconvinced by the claim that IQ is largely heritable. "To say that these data close the case on environmental effects on IQ is a scientific farce," she concluded. "Those who persist in maintaining that an accurate heritability estimate can be obtained from these data and who extend the estimate to discuss racial differences in IQ . . . should question their own motivation and commitment to a dispassionate search for full understanding." The data for personality development was even more questionable, she charged. "Magnify every problem in the IQ data—tests, sampling bias, and so forth—a hundredfold for the measurement of personality difference," she wrote, charging that the validity of all personality tests is open to question.

Farber found in the twin literature reason to believe that environment played a substantial role in the formation of individual personalities. "Family influences show clearly in attitudes, values, choice of mate, and in presence of nonpsychotic psychiatric symptomatology. The cultural or regional influences transmitted by the family and social network also are present and probably show in general personality traits ranging from emotional expressivity to drinking habits . . . everything in these data points toward the massive and perhaps predominant influence of family and culture on attitudes and psychological traits."

The paradox that Farber discovered, however, was that, as a group, "the more time MZ twins spend with no contact with each other, the more similar they seem to become," which directly counters the environmental argument advanced by Kamin. Early in the Minnesota study, Bouchard also got results indicating that separated twins were sometimes more similar than twins raised together. "You could argue that the twins reared together, because of the presence of each other, forced themselves apart. They differentiate. Whereas, if they were reared apart, they couldn't care less about this," he says. As the number of twins tested increased, however, this idea became harder to support. Bouchard now believes that twins reared apart and twins reared together are "about the same" in most measured tests. Separated twins who were separated later or who have spent more time together have no more difference in their IQs than those who were separated at birth and have practically never met.

Among the twins who came to Minnesota, there was a British pair with a wide disparity in education and family background. One of the twins was raised by working-class parents and left school at sixteen. She spoke with a distinct Cockney accent. Her twin was raised by a university professor and was educated in private schools. Their difference in IQ, however, was less than the average difference between MZ twins raised together. According to David Lykken, the largest IQ difference among the separated twins in the Minnesota sample was found in a pair of older men. One had been adopted by illiterate parents and had quit school at the age of thirteen; his brother, whose IQ was 29 points higher, was raised by better-educated parents and had gone into the military. Lykken theorizes that it may be easier to lower IQ, by suppressing education and stimulation, than to raise it. He also wonders if the lower-IQ twin may have suffered some kind of brain damage at birth. In any case, it is clear that the overwhelming flow of data about the near-perfect correlation of intelligence, personality, and behavior among identical twins masks vivid distinctions within individual pairs.

Another common critique of the classic comparison of identical versus fraternal twins is that identical twins by definition look more alike; their parents are also more likely to treat them similarly and dress them alike. "There is no great imagination required to see how such a difference between MZs and DZs might produce the reported difference in IQ correlations," Kamin wrote with two other prominent and persistent critics, Steven Rose, a neurobiologist at the Open University in England, and Richard C. Lewontin, an evolutionary geneticist at Harvard. Their 1984 book, *Not in Our Genes: Biology, Ideology, and Human Nature,* assailed the entire field of behavior genetics. Kamin points to a study in which photographs of MZ twin pairs were sorted by judges on the basis of which twins looked more nearly identical; those who were most similar in looks were also somewhat more alike in IQ.* It is likely, says Kamin, that identical twins spend more time studying together, and that they are often treated as a single unit by their teachers, so it is unsurprising that they would receive similar grades and similar scores on intelligence tests. "When I first got interested in this, the following thought occurred," Kamin recalls. "Try to imagine a family in which there is a pair of twins plus a third kid. Suppose you try to get IQ correlations between the third kid and either one of the twins—you'd expect a correlation of 0.50. But the correlation is amazingly small." The point, says Kamin, is that "twins form a closed society. The third kid has a much lower resemblance to them than he would have if either of the others were not twins."† These arguments don't address the situation of reared-apart twins, but it is certainly possible to imagine that reared-apart identical twins would be treated somewhat alike by their adoptive families because of their physical similarity.

Other kinds of family studies have found lower genetic correlations for intelligence: between 0.40 and 0.70. At the lower end of that scale, one could expect the environment to play a much more decisive role, especially as one grows older. All the factors that go into cre-

*Most studies that have examined the degree of physical resemblance in identical twins have found little or no correlation to similarities in personality or ability. Indeed, parents rated MZ twins who were most frequently confused for each other as least alike in behavior.

†In fact, the Louisville Twin Study tested Kamin's thought experiment in 1978, matching the cognitive performance of twins with the performance of non-twin siblings at the same age. The Louisville team found that fraternal twins were more like each other than their non-twin sibling at age three, but these differences had disappeared by the age of six.

ating what we term the "environment"—one's family, culture, level of education, occupation, nutrition, health, exposure to stress, and so on—naturally increase with the storehouse of life experiences. A team of Swedish, British, and American scientists under the leadership of Dr. Gerald E. McClearn recently concluded a two-year study of 240 elderly Swedish twin pairs, all born before the First World War. They were given a range of tests for mental ability. Identical twins were much more alike than fraternal twins of the same sex—no surprise—but what seems so confounding is that the elderly identical twins were more alike in mental functioning than younger identical twins. The role of heredity in determining intelligence only seems to grow with age,* and yet a lifetime of living different lives in different environments apparently had served only to make the identical twins more similar, whereas the fraternal twins became less alike over time.

The most recent and possibly the most substantive criticism of twin studies was advanced in a 1997 letter to the British journal *Nature* by Bernie Devlin, a psychiatrist at the University of Pittsburgh School of Medicine, and two statisticians at Carnegie Mellon University. Behavioral geneticists had discovered a puzzling inconsistency in the data on intelligence derived from twins reared apart and twins reared together. When one calculated the heritability of intelligence based on separated twins, it was about 0.70; but when one calculated the same data on twins who grew up in the same environment, the heritability of intelligence dropped to about 0.50. The behavioral geneticists assumed that the difference was accounted for by the fact that nearly all

*The McClearn team found that heritability of general cognitive ability increased from infancy (about twenty percent) to childhood (forty percent) to adolescence (fifty percent) to adulthood (sixty percent).

the reared-apart twins who have ever been studied were middle-aged adults, whereas the IQ correlations for twins reared together were based largely on data that came from children and adolescents. If, indeed, identical twins grow to be more alike over time, then logically this "age effect" would explain the fact that the adult intelligence of reared-apart twins is more similar than that of reared-together twin children.

Devlin and his colleagues, Michael Daniels and Kathryn Roeder, thought that there must be another explanation. Age does not seem to affect personality, so why would it affect intelligence? Devlin also observed that twins who have been reared apart are said to have no common environment, but obviously that's not true—they shared the environment of the womb. Devlin claims that most studies of intelligence have presumed that the prenatal environment has a negligible influence on the development of intelligence, and yet a child's height or birth weight, for instance, can be significantly affected by the health of the mother during her pregnancy. Moreover, prenatal exposure to substances such as alcohol, lead, drugs, and cigarettes has been shown to lower IQ, just as good nutrition has been shown to raise it.

The Pittsburgh team postulated that this "maternal effect" accounts for the difference between the heritability correlations of intelligence between reared-apart and reared-together twins. They built a statistical model to analyze 212 previous studies of intelligence correlations that had been derived through kinship and adoption studies. They found that the maternal effect accounted for twenty percent of the variation of intelligence among twins and five percent among ordinary siblings—a rather extraordinary figure, which if true would lower the heritability estimates of intelligence by quite a margin. Indeed, the Pittsburgh team calculated that the broad heritability of intelligence was about 0.48—giving a slight majority to the influence of the environment, including the prenatal environment. Such a figure would be far too low to support Jensen's argument, reiterated and expanded by Herrnstein and Murray in *The Bell Curve,* that the intermarriage of highly educated, intelligent people will lead inevitably to separate castes based on IQ scores. It is also considerably lower than the 0.66 figure that Bouchard cites as a consensus for all twin studies. "Overall, the study results have two implications," says Devlin. "A new model may be required regarding the influence of genes and environment on cognitive function, and interventions aimed at improving the prenatal environment could lead to a significant increase in the population's IQ."

Much of Devlin's information is arrived at by comparing fraternal twins with ordinary siblings. Despite the fact that on average fraternal twins are no more genetically alike than ordinary brothers and sisters, each having about half their genes in common, fraternal twins show much more similarity in intelligence. That increased similarity, says Devlin, is the maternal effect—the experience of sharing the same womb serves to make twins more alike than ordinary siblings. However, the experience of sharing the womb also tends to make twins different from each other. They compete for space and nutrition and even blood, which can create striking dissimilarities—so much so that many twin researchers believe that their data on heritability actually underestimates the heritability for the population as a whole.

Bouchard disputes Devlin's analysis on several grounds. For one, he points to studies demonstrating that fraternal twins actually grow to be less alike in their intelligence as they age—more like ordinary brothers and sisters—so that whatever effect Devlin is demonstrating disappears as the twins become adults. "If they were just drawing conclusions about the sample they worked with, which is heavily children, I'd say, 'Well, who knows?' But I know there's information about older adults, I know that these common family environmental influences disappear and that the postulate of maternal effects runs counter to all the work done by people who've studied prenatal effects. And so I just don't believe that this is the best model. They may be right in the long run. I just don't think so." The diminishing effect of prenatal experience is a quandary that the environmentalists acknowledge but have been unable to solve.

A more sinister charge is that the separated twins are making up stories in order to get into the press. "I don't blame the twins," says Kamin. "There's enormous implied pressure on them to exaggerate the degree of their separation. Nobody would be interested in them, they would not appear in the newspapers, they would not appear on TV shows and so on, if they said, 'Yeah, we saw quite a bit of each other and we went to the same schools.' If they convince other people and themselves that they saw very little of one another, then they're going to be valuable scientific resources and people will beat a path to their door. I think it is beyond cavil that these twins tend to gild the lily." Kamin points out that there is an economic interest as well: several of the separated twins, including the Jims and Jack and Oskar, have signed movie or book deals. Kamin claimed to have spoken to Jim Springer's mother, who he says admitted to him that the twins had met repeatedly in Florida when they were young but kept it a secret from Springer's father. "Now that appears, of course, in all the apocryphal literature about this as some mysterious things in the genes led the two of them to go each year to Saint Petersburg. I know she spoke to me about the fact that she had to keep these meetings secret from her husband." Kamin said he had notes of the conversation, but when asked to produce them, he found that there was no reference to the twins' meeting or the mothers' having known each other. "I don't know whether I was told or I deduced it," he says now. Jim Springer says such meetings never occurred.

"God could appear to me in a dream and tell me the outcome of a perfect twin study, and my question to God would be, 'Okay, now that I know that the heritability is 0.469327, what do I do with it? Tell me what that tells me,' " says Lewontin, one of Kamin's coauthors. He criticizes the statistical practice of correlation, which implies causal relationships between genes and behavior that may have nothing in common. "If I look at people who knit and people who don't knit, I will make the following discovery: that almost everybody who knits has two X chromosomes and people who don't knit have one X and one Y. Now, how can it be that having two X chromosomes makes you knit? Well, we know the answer to that. Having two X chromosomes makes you into a woman. In our society it is cultural—purely cultural—that women knit. If we had looked at exactly the same problem in eighteenth-century England, we would have found that all knitters have one X chromosome and one Y, because it was men who did knitting—it was an economically important occupation. We wouldn't want to say there are genes for knitting on the X chromosome, but we understand that there are genes that make you into a female, which in the present historical circumstance has as a consequence that it's okay for you to knit."

It is certainly true that statistics can be used to associate unrelated matters. Daniel Patrick Moynihan, a

United States senator who is also a distinguished sociologist, rather famously made the case on the subject of IQ, when Southern intellectuals were asserting white-race superiority. Moynihan found a high correlation between intelligence and proximity to the Canadian border. The further south one traveled, he demonstrated, the lower the IQ. As is the case with race, however, the variation within a region is so great that geography is virtually worthless as a predictor of individual IQ.

The statistical detective work that behavioral geneticists have done has already prompted an extraordinary reevaluation of the architecture of the human personality. And yet Lewontin has claimed that "nothing we can know about the genetics of human behavior can have any implications for human society," a statement that is perhaps best described as wishful thinking on his part. Lewontin and his coauthors Kamin and Rose are socialists who believe that the rise of biological determinism has led to the political ascendancy of the New Right. They are no doubt correct. Society will organize itself around its beliefs of how human nature operates in the world. "The consequences of determinism reach out beyond theory," Steven Rose wrote, perhaps despairingly, in *Nature* in 1995. "If the homeless or depressed are so because of a flaw in their biology, their condition cannot be the fault of society, albeit a humane society will attempt, pharmacologically or otherwise, to alleviate their distress. This 'victim blaming' generates in its turn a sort of fatalism among those it stigmatizes."

As the views of the environmentalists lose favor, the politics that have been built upon their assumptions crumble. There has simply been nothing on the environmental side to counter the power of twin and adoption studies. "When I point to the weaknesses of behavioral genetics studies, I'm not saying there are a whole set of marvelous environmental studies," Kamin concedes. "We don't know what in the environment affects IQ. There's just not a good study on the family environment."

So far, the molecular evidence that would buttress the statistical studies of behavioral genetics has been slow in coming. As scientists map the human genome, they have been able to identify a few disorders that are caused by a single gene, such as cystic fibrosis, phenylketonuria, and Huntington's disease. In several cases, scientists have trumpeted genetic markers for such things as manic depression or schizophrenia and have then quietly withdrawn their findings.

The brain depends upon enzymes for the neurochemical process we call thinking, and those enzymes are created by genes. From a biochemical perspective, there is an obvious genetic contribution to intelligence, but no single gene that makes one person smarter than another. Instead, more than half of the body's 100,000 genes donate in some way to the general fund of intelligence. Robert Plomin, a behavioral geneticist of the Institute of Psychiatry in London, who at that time was at Pennsylvania State University, examined two groups of children, one with high IQs and another with low IQs, to see if there were particular markers that were in or near genes thought to be associated with cognition. He found five markers that had significant associations with differences in intelligence, but four of them failed to be replicated in an independent sample.

Perhaps the most successful example of twin studies leading to molecular discovery is the example of Tourette's syndrome, a bizarre neurological disorder characterized by chronic tics, sometimes violent twitching, intrusive thoughts, and the uttering of repetitious, meaningless phrases. Tourette's runs in families and has all the characteristics of a genetic disease, and yet the search of the human genome has so far yielded no obvious genetic markers for the disorder. Daniel Weinberger, chief of the Clinical Disorders Branch at the National Institute of Mental Health in Baltimore, studied five sets of identical twins. In each set, one twin meets the so-called "300-yard diagnosis," which means that his symptoms are so apparent that an observer can diagnose them at that distance, whereas the other twin has less severe symptoms. When the researchers examined the brains of the twins, they found that the more affected twin had extremely sensitive receptors for the brain chemical dopamine. Dopamine affects the section of the brain called the caudate nucleus, the region where motor actions are planned. Because each set of twins has identical genes, the researchers reason that the cause of the difference in their dopamine receptors may have to do with birth trauma—it was usually true that the twin with the lower birth weight grew up to be the more severely affected—or else the stress of different life events. In either case, it appears that there is a genetic basis for the disease, but it requires an environmental trigger to awaken its catastrophic potential.

Alcoholism also runs in families, and identical twins are far more alike in respect to their drinking behavior than fraternal twins. Moreover, identical twins who have been raised apart are about as alike in their drinking as identical twins raised together. This suggests, as strongly as any other twin studies, that alcoholism is an inherited disorder. In 1990, researchers at the University of Texas Health Science Center at San Antonio claimed to have linked the D-2 dopamine receptor gene to alcoholism—the same location where scientists found the discordance for Tourette's syndrome—but other scientists failed to replicate the finding. Even if there is an alcoholic gene, however, it is clear that environment influences much of drinking behavior. Children of alcoholics who have been adopted into families where drinking is not a problem rarely become alcoholics themselves; such cases seem to depend upon the stability of the adopting family. Twin studies correlating drinking behavior with religious affiliation found that alcoholism was five times higher in people with no religious affiliation than in the most fundamentalist group. Presumably Muslims and Amish people would carry at least some genetic vulnerability for alcoholism, if there is such a thing, but alcoholism is rarely a problem in cultures where people are simply forbidden to drink.

Similarly, divorce has a strong heritable component, at least in the United States. However, divorce is not tolerated in Amish societies; and in traditional Muslim societies men can have multiple wives and may divorce simply by renouncing the marriage. In such environments, genes that might influence divorce would have wildly different opportunities to express themselves. Many studies have shown that children of divorced parents have more emotional problems and perform more poorly in school, and eventually get more divorces than children of parents who stay together—but is that because of the divorce? Or do the children also inherit genes for personalities and behavior that may later lead to their own wrecked relationships?

To take another controversial example, homosexuality may be partly genetically driven. There is ample support for this from neuroscientists, who have found female brain structures in male transsexuals, and from molecular geneticists, who think they have isolated a "gay gene" on the X chromosome. Michael Bailey, a psychologist at Northwestern University, and Richard

C. Pillard, a psychiatrist at the Family Studies Laboratory of Boston University School of Medicine, studied 161 gay men, each of whom had an identical or fraternal twin or an adopted brother. They found fifty-two percent of the identical twins of gay men were also gay, compared with twenty-two percent of the fraternal twins and eleven percent of the adopted brothers. Bailey did a separate study of Australian twins, however, and found that the chances of a gay twin having a gay brother were only twenty percent among identicals and nearly zero among fraternals. In Bouchard's reared-apart twin sample there are two sets of twins with homosexual men; in one set both twins are gay, in the other only one is. A larger sample of more than ten thousand twins found that the heritability for sexual orientation in women was nearly fifty percent, but in men it was zero.

Even if homosexuality in men is shown to be, for instance, thirty percent heritable, what, exactly, is inherited? "The fair thing to say is that nobody knows," says Pillard. "Is it a propensity to like somebody who is sort of the same as you versus somebody who's different, or to like a man versus a woman, or to be very sensitive or what? To me that's the payoff question. What is it doing up there in that little brain that's making you different? What's the mechanism for that? It's hard even to speculate because we don't know that much about how genes affect behavior."

One reason is that research has been discouraged. When Dutch scientists announced that they had found a gene linked to aggression, they were denounced for even considering violent behavior as a genetic expression. The U.S. National Institutes of Health canceled a planned 1992 conference at the University of Maryland, "Genetic Factors in Crime," and scaled back its research on causes of violence. (The conference finally took place three years later.) Again and again, when genetic research turns toward human nature, rather than simple biology, politics swamps the discussion and often sinks the research efforts. In most instances, the only proof of genetic influence on personality and behavior still comes from twin and adoption studies. As a result, there is a magical air about them, because they traffic in taboo ideas, demonstrating effects without revealing causes.

6

Twin Mysteries

In 1973 Jerry L. Hall, of the George Washington University Medical Center, reported that he had succeeded in cloning human embryos, using a method that had already been perfected with animals. Dr. Hall merely split the embryo, then at the stage of only a few cells, into two or three parts. Each lump of cells developed normally into twin or triplet embryos. The object of the experiment was to make more embryos available for women who were undergoing in vitro fertilization. Those embryos that were not implanted in the womb were discarded, but they could easily have been frozen and used later, perhaps in other women. Thus the study of twins gains a weird pertinence for the future, as we envision twins separated not only by distance but by time as well.

Whether the clones are formed by splitting embryos or by some other technique, like the one used by Dr. Ian Wilmut at the Roslin Institute in Scotland to clone an adult sheep, they will share the same genes—just like identical twins—and similar problems of identity, but they will create new puzzles of kinship. For instance, an adult female who clones herself creates not only her child but her twin sister. The child's genetic parents are the people she would otherwise identify as her grandparents.

Clones may in some respects be more identical to each other than naturally occurring identical twins. Twin fetuses can do a lot of harm to each other, and clones grown separately would not have to endure the competition in the womb. Also, there may be something about the splitting process that results in twins that may also cause birth defects. Mice embryos that have been artificially divided and allowed to develop tend to be weaker than normally developed mice. It is possible—in fact, likely—that clones could be created without the same liabilities that attend the twinning process.

During the broad public debate about the morality of cloning human beings, clones have repeatedly been described as nothing more than identical twins, as if that robbed the debate of its mystery. The truth is that the twinning process is much less well understood than cloning, which is a rather simple procedure. In spite of the burst of twin-based scholarship in recent years, much that is commonly believed to be true about twinning is either wrong or in dispute. It is not clear, for instance, whether twinning is a kind of birth defect or, contrarily, whether birth defects are caused by twinning (or if, indeed, either has anything to do with the other). We don't know what significance, if any, to attach to the elevated incidence of left-handedness among both kinds of twins. It is not even certain whether fraternal twins always come from two eggs or sometimes from one that has split before fertilization, creating a third kind of twin. We are only now learning that twins are different in particular ways from singletons (their teeth are less symmetrical, for example), but we don't know why or what that means. In sum, we don't know who twins are or how twins happen. We only presume to know what they tell us about who *we* are.

So much depends on a phenomenon about which we know so little. Even the prevalence of twins is a subject of puzzlement and controversy. With the increasing use of ultrasound to detect early pregnancies, we now know that twinning is a far more common occurrence than anyone had previously imagined. Although only about one out of eighty or ninety live births produces twins, at least one-eighth of all natural pregnancies begin as twins. Many of us singletons, in other words, began life as something more—as part of a pair.

The use of sonography to detect pregnancy dates from 1957, but it didn't become widespread until the late seventies. By that time, we already knew more about the ocean floor and the dark side of the moon than we did about embryogenesis. Before ultrasound, it was impossible to diagnose accurately twin pregnancies, and most multiple births came as a surprise. As ultrasound became more common and increasingly more sophisticated, however, doctors began having the unnerving experience of viewing twin embryos one month, only to find a singleton the next time they looked. What was happening? In 1980, at the Third International Congress on Twin Studies in Jerusalem, this question was raised, and one of the participants cried out, "Vanishing twins!" thus giving a name to a phenomenon that has caused as much confusion as excitement.

Usually the only external sign of a vanished twin is vaginal bleeding. More advanced ultrasound equipment, including vaginal ultrasound, high-speed scanners, and color Doppler (the same kind of radar apparatus meteorologists use to track the movement of weather), has been able to detect multiple pregnancies as early as five weeks after conception. A 1992 Israeli study, using transvaginal sonography, diagnosed eighty-eight multiple gestations among women who had undergone ovulation induction. Of the fifty-four twin pregnancies detected in this group between five and six weeks, fifty-one resulted in the birth of singletons and three were spontaneously aborted; the rest had vanished. There were also twenty-six triplet gestations, producing twelve pairs of twins, twelve singletons, and two complete miscarriages; five quadruplet pregnancies, which produced three triplets, two twins, and a singleton; and three quintuplet pregnancies, two of which were deliberately reduced by doctors to a set of triplets and a set of twins, but there were three vanished fetuses as well. Two different studies found that the frequency of twins among abortions is three times higher than the frequency of twins at birth.

"People are picking up twin pregnancies the size of garden peas. They're seeing a lot more twins than they ever knew were there," according to Charles E. Boklage, a geneticist at East Carolina University School of Medicine and a well-known maverick in the world of twin biology. Boklage has a knack for uncovering paradoxical data that undermine many of the commonplace assumptions people still harbor about twins. "The so-called phenomenon of the 'vanishing twin syndrome' is neither phenomenal nor a syndrome," Boklage contends. "It is much too common to be considered phenomenal, and it occurs for too many reasons to be considered any kind of syndrome." He says that most pregnancies, whether multiple or singleton, fail in any case, so it is not as surprising as it seems that twins often disappear. "Somewhere in the vicinity of twelve to fifteen percent of us—and that's a *minimum* estimate—are walking around thinking we're singletons when in fact we're only the big half," says Boklage. He estimates that for every set of twins born alive, there are at least six singletons born who are sole survivors of twin conceptions. "Now, the implications of this are profound. A huge fraction of the population are products of twin pregnancies, and therefore are presumably associated with all the things that known twin pregnancies are associated with in terms of malformations and extra risks."*

Twins are far more susceptible to the birth defects, spontaneous mutations, and vascular problems that threaten early life. Simply being a twin is stressful and raises the odds against survival because of the competition for space and nutrients. If an embryo disappears in the first trimester, it has probably been absorbed by the placenta or by the other twin, with little or no evidence that it ever existed, except for the tiny image it may once have left on ultrasound. A careful examination of the placenta after birth will sometimes reveal a nodule that turns out to be the remains of a vanished twin.

The death of one twin poses a real threat to the other. Identical twins share the same circulation in the womb, and the death of one could cause a blood clot to pass into the survivor, causing heart damage or developmental problems of exactly the sort twins are famous for. Cysts, called teratomas, composed of bits of hair and teeth and fetal bones, are sometimes discovered in adults. Either they are errant cells that have reverted to a primitive embryological state or they are the remnant of a vanished identical twin. Dead fetuses have also been found inside living children. There is a well-known case in 1949 of such a "fetus-in-fetu," in which five fetuses were removed from the brain of an infant girl in Philadelphia; several less spectacular cases have been reported since, including a six-pound fetus found during the autopsy of an elderly man. These events are probably accidents of timing during early pregnancy. Identical

*Of course, many of the problems of multiple births are associated with late stages of pregnancy—crowding and premature birth, for instance—and they would not be a feature of vanished-twin syndrome.

twinning is thought to occur on or before the fourteenth day after conception. If the division happens early in that cycle, the embryos will be in separate placentas, like nearly all fraternal twins. By the end of the fourth day, the chorion, which is the outer placental membrane, will have formed, and if the zygote divides after that time, as is the case with two-thirds of MZ twins, they develop in a single placenta. If the division occurs between the fifth and the eighth days, the twins will still be encased in separate amniotic sacs, but if they divide after the eighth day there will be nothing between them. Half of these late-splitting twins die, often strangling in each other's umbilical cords. It is thought that by the twelfth day the division is likely to be incomplete, resulting conjoined or Siamese twins, which occur in about one out of 400 MZ births,* fetus-in-fetu, and teratomas. These are, however, only theories. One can also make the case that the twinning process got stuck at the beginning and never advanced. These abnormalities are far more prevalent in girls than in boys, since male twins (like all boys) are more likely to miscarry.

Because all twins compete in the womb for space and nutrition, the experiences of twins before birth are considerably different from those of singletons. "Twins also compete physically," says Louis Keith, the head of the Center for Study of Multiple Birth in Chicago and the editor of *Multipregnancy: Epidemiology, Gestation, and Perinatal Outcome.* One doctor on his staff at Northwestern University Medical School observed twin fetuses fighting. "One punched the other and the other looked startled," says Keith. "On another occasion, when he was looking with the ultrasound at triplets,

*The estimates for the overall frequency of conjoined twin births vary significantly, from one out of every 33,000 births to one out of 175,000.

two of them were kissing as clear as day. Among multiples, there is intrauterine life. They do fight. They do kiss."

There is considerable evidence that when one twin dies the survivor can suffer lifelong feelings of guilt. The loss may be felt most deeply by those whose twin died at birth or shortly afterward. Elvis Presley's twin brother, Jesse, was stillborn, a deeply affecting event in Elvis's life; one has to wonder how American popular culture might have been different had his twin survived. Elizabeth Bryan, who is director of the Multiple Births Foundation in London, set up the Lone Twin Network to provide support for survivors coping with their grief. She says, "I've met quite a number of people who only discovered their twin was stillborn— that is, they only discovered that they were a twin at all—at some adult occasion such as they were about to get married, or their first child was on the way, and their mother suddenly said, 'Your twin died and I never told you.' Several of them said that the news came as a profound relief. For the first time they understood the loss they had felt all their lives. Of course, one could argue that their loss could be explained by being brought up by bereaved parents who were hiding something." Lately Bryan reports seeing a number of people who claim to be survivors of vanished twins. Already, as one might have guessed, there are psychotherapies designed to regress patients into the womb so that they can get in touch with their vanished twin. Elizabeth Noble, founder of the Maternal and Child Health Center in Cambridge, Massachusetts, and author of *Having Twins,* underwent primal therapy in Australia and claims to have discovered that her interest in twins came from being a surviving twin. "To this day I hold a clear image and feeling of a disappearing embryo," she writes. She has now written a memoir of her intrauterine life called *Inside Experiences: From Conception through Birth.*

David Teplica, a plastic surgeon in Chicago, also has come to believe that he might be the survivor of a twin pair, although he tells his story with evident embarrassment. "It just seems so *National Enquirer*—'Doctor Searches for Dead Twin,' " says Teplica, who is also an acclaimed photographer. "It's been since my early teens that I was obsessed with the idea of twinning. I would read everything about twins. I started photographing twins in about 1988. At first it was not an obsession, it was just fun." He got to know Louis Keith and his identical twin, Donald, who is a defense contractor in Washington. Through them he turned his hobby into a more formal project. The following year, he went with the Keiths to the annual twin festival in Twinsburg, Ohio. "It was incredible—for the first couple of hours. Perhaps if you're a twin, it's incredible for a couple of days. You very quickly start feeling like you're alone. It's weird. Of course, it's a gold mine for researchers, but after a while I thought, Boy, I'm just a singleton."

Since then, Teplica has compiled an archive of approximately 6,000 twin portraits, while conducting his own twin study. As a plastic surgeon, he is professionally interested in the aesthetics of the human face. In every twin pair, one is usually considered more attractive than the other. (How that could be is a fascinating subject in itself. Because of their genetic identity, the nuances that make twins look different must be largely environmental in origin—for instance, subtle differences in fetal development and the birth process.) By having students pick the more attractive twin from various pairs of photos, Teplica hopes to measure the anatomic variances that make up the standards of beauty. "There have been fascinating things that have come up as a part of the whole process of collecting these images," he says. "It's now clear to me that almost all secondary skin characteristics on the head and face, and probably elsewhere, are genetically predetermined. For example, freckle patterns, hair whorls, the first gray hairs, the first wrinkles on the human face, even the development of acne on the same location on the nose at exactly the same time—all these things seem to be in some way genetically predetermined. It's frightening. Why else would two identical twins from upstate New York get exactly the same three little crow's-feet at the corners of the eyes? Why would two women from Texas develop basal-cell carcinoma in exactly the same spot on their left ears within a year of each other? Why would two young men from Ohio have the same extra hairs on their cheeks and the same cupped-ear deformities? How can it be that two cell clusters that were separated fifty years ago have enough information to determine where your blackheads would develop when you are fifty or sixty years old? It's really very scary."

After a year or so of Teplica's collaboration with the Keith twins, Donald Keith asked him, "David, why are you so fascinated with twins? Maybe you *are* one."

Teplica laughed. "Donald, I'm *not* a twin," he responded.

But the next time his mother came to visit, Teplica asked if there was any chance that he was a twin. "She turned white," he recalls. "She paused, and said, 'David, I'd never thought you'd hear this.' She proceeded to tell me how she had tried to get pregnant for many years, and when she finally became pregnant she was so large, put on so much weight so quickly, that her physician told her she would be delivering twins. But then in the fourth month, she had some cramping, passed some tissue, had some bleeding, was put on bed rest, and delivered only me. Now, that was before the days of ultrasound, but every indication was that she did have a twin pregnancy."

Charles Boklage believes that most malformed children who were born as singletons actually may be the products of twin pregnancies. This may also be true of left-handers, who are more common among twins.* He cites another interesting phenomenon, which, although it has rarely been detected, may not be at all uncommon. "It is possible that I am twins. By that I mean that two different embryos went together to make one body. We know that occasionally happens, but it is almost never detected except in blood banks. I think it is actually much more common than that. I can tell you with complete certainty that some of us are twins who are walking around in a single body." Such a creature is called a chimera, after the mythological Greek monster that had the head of a lion, the body of a goat, and the tail of a serpent. Chimeras are easily produced in the laboratory. "We've had thousands of experiments with rats and mice in which we take part of a mouse embryo and stick it in a rat embryo," says Boklage. "We've done it between sexes and between species. They never make twins. They always fuse into single embryos and come out part rat, part mouse; part male, part female; part sheep, part goat. The forces involved in embryogenesis simply overpower the differences in their origins. I'm sure there are creatures too far apart to put together, like a mouse and a chicken. But when these events occur in human development, it simply goes on." Chimeras sometimes happen in nature when littermates

*Interestingly, the voodoo culture anticipated the vanishing twin idea long before it became a subject of legitimate scientific interest. In Haiti a child is counted as a "twin" if he is born with webbed fingers, a sign, it is believed, that he has "eaten" his sibling in the womb.

fuse together. The fact that this happens in humans was only discovered when donors in blood banks were found to be carrying two different blood types; it could mean that fraternal twins merged in the womb. Most human chimeras are to some extent hermaphrodites, with ambiguous genitalia. Of course, there is no way to discover if identical twins have merged, since their genes and blood types are the same. In these cases, the twins don't vanish, they amalgamate.

When an infant twin girl, a year and a half old, recently appeared in the Department of Pediatrics at the British Columbia Children's Hospital in Vancouver suffering from chronic lung infections, Judith Hall routinely checked for cystic fibrosis. By analyzing the chloride level in her sweat, Dr. Hall got a positive diagnosis. "We then decided it was time to check the twin," says Hall. As it happens, when these twins were born their obstetrician carefully examined the membranes of the placenta to determine their zygosity. There was a single chorionic sac, so the doctor assumed that the girls must be identical. And yet, when Hall tested the eighteen-month-old twin for cystic fibrosis, there was no sign of the disease. "We then decided to do blood studies, looking for common mutations that occur in cystic fibrosis—and they weren't there in *either* twin! So we scratched our heads. We then decided to take a bit of skin, and when we did that, the kid with cystic fibrosis had the common mutations and the other didn't." This was a terrific muddle. The other twin was not even a carrier of cystic fibrosis—no evidence of the gene at all. DNA tests showed that the girls were not, in fact, MZ twins. Apparently they were the result of two separate acts of conception, but the zygotes implanted so close to each other in the uterus that the placentas fused. Further testing showed that the diseased twin was carrying the blood of the healthy twin. They had evidently shared the same circulation in the womb, which is common among identicals, but rare among fraternals. "They were two separate creatures, but they shared their blood in the placenta at such an early age that one twin actually took over for the abnormal twin, so its blood was healthy but the rest of its body had cystic fibrosis," says Hall. "That's a chimera."

There does seem to be a connection between birth defects and twinning, but researchers still disagree as to which causes the other and whether the defects are confined mainly to identicals or are characteristic of both kinds of twins. Of course, it could also be true that twinning and birth defects are both caused by some other trait. The malformations most often associated with twins are heart defects, spina bifida, and cystic fibrosis. Boklage has observed that these same malformations are also found at a higher rate than expected in their non-twin siblings and offspring. But the same is true for left-handedness: thirty-five percent of identical twins are left-handed, double the rate of the general population. To add to the mystery, this association of twins, left-handedness, and malformations of other non-twin family members is just as true for fraternal as for identical twins. And yet the most fundamental proposition of twin science is that fraternal and identical twinning are entirely separate processes. Fraternal twins are supposed to happen when two eggs are separately fertilized. They can be conceived at different times during the same menstrual cycle and even by different fathers, which leads to the occasional situation where there are twins of different racial or ethnic origin. Some fraternal twins are so different in their birth weight that it is possible they were conceived during different menstrual cycles. Identical twins happen when a single egg is fertilized, then in the course of the development the zygote divides. The process of fraternal twinning, on the other hand, is not supposed to have anything to do with splitting. Genetically, DZ twins are assumed to be no more alike than ordinary siblings who are born separately. These suppositions are at the heart of twin studies. If, as Boklage was suggesting, the two forms of twinning have something in common, and if both kinds of twins were more like each other than they were like singletons, then the thousands of twin studies that seek to determine which traits are inherited and which are environmental would be called into question.

Boklage decided to do a study on twins' teeth. "I took the teeth as a way to ask questions about building a head," he says. "The teeth are a subsystem of the head. Bike a brain, teeth grow in a highly coordinated fashion between the left and right halves, and they come from the same top layer of the embryo as the whole nervous system. Back when the embryo was a flat disc, they were in the same cells as the future brain. I first found that the teeth of identical and fraternal twins were different—they were so different I could tell you whether an individual came from an identical twin pair without seeing the other twin. When I first started doing that, I thought fraternal twins were ordinary people." Twins' teeth were on the whole less regular and symmetrical than the teeth of singletons, and the teeth of identical twins were less regular than those of fraternals. The differences in dentition suggest to Boklage that there might be other differences between twins and singletons as well. "The simple fact is we have never known enough about twins and twinning to do such studies right," he says. For instance, there might be a third type of twinning, in which fraternal twins derive from a single egg, one that splits *before* conception, so that the same egg is fertilized twice. That would confound comparisons between identicals and fraternals, undermining the whole structure of behavior genetics.

There was a way of testing at least part of Boklage's hypothesis. In Belgium, Catherine Derom and her colleagues at the Center for Human Genetics in the Catholic University of Leuven were looking into the relationship between artificially induced ovulation and multiple births. The connection between the two was well known and easily explained. Artificial ovulation made more eggs available to be fertilized. Therefore any increase in twins should be accounted for by the fertilization of the superfluous eggs. In short, all the twins should be fraternal. Derom reasoned that if there were any connection at all between fraternal and identical twins, then there would also be an increase of identical twins among the population of children born after artificially induced ovulation. She examined twins born by artificial induction in East Flanders between 1964 and 1985. To the astonishment of nearly everyone in the field, Derom discovered that identical twins were being born at a rate three times higher than normal. She was at a loss to provide a satisfactory explanation.

"Some of the things we don't know yet are whether all the disappeared twins are monozygous or dizygous," says Judith Hall. "We don't know whether the increased incidence of congenital anomalies that is reported in all twins is primarily in monozygous twins or whether it is actually found in both kinds of twins. We still have a lot of work to do in establishing whether twins come from one egg or two eggs. Now that we have DNA markers, I think we'll get much better data about what are the differences between dizygous and monozygous twins. In general, it's thought that dizygous twins are caused by high levels of hormones that make you ovulate. By contrast, nobody has a clue why monozygous twins happen."

The rate of dizygotic twinning varies wildly among various countries and ethnic groups, ranging from a low of six twin pairs per 1,000 births in Japan to forty-five pairs per 1,000 in Nigeria. The tendency to have fraternal twins appears to be both genetic and environmental. Broadly speaking, Orientals have the lowest rate, Caucasians an intermediate rate, and Africans the highest rate of twinning, but there are remarkable differences within populations that are genetically very much alike. The Yoruba tribe in Nigeria are the world champions of twinning: as many as one out of eleven Yorubans is a twin—far more than other tribes in the region—although the rate of identical twinning is no greater than in Europe or the United States. The high rate of fraternal twinning among the Yoruba may be accounted for in part by diet. The tribe eats a species of yam particularly high in estrogen, which causes an increase in follicle-stimulating hormone (FSH), which may cause higher rates of ovulation. When the Yorubans move to the city, the twinning rate declines, presumably because their diet changes, although there is also a correlation between high twinning rates and agricultural labor, for whatever reason.

Twinning has also been shown to be genetically influenced and carried through the maternal line, although in several families the trait appears to have been passed along through the father's genes as well (this point is still hotly disputed, however, like so much of twin research). Tall, heavy women give birth to twins more often than short, thin women, perhaps because they are better nourished. Older women are far more likely to conceive twins than are younger women, probably due to higher rates of FSH secretion. The twinning rate begins to fall after age thirty-seven, which may be the result of the increased likelihood of spontaneous abortions.

Twins also happen more frequently to unwed mothers—forty percent more often than to married mothers, according to one Swedish study. The explanation offered is that irregularity of intercourse allows the awaiting egg to go unfertilized for a longer period of time; as the egg begins to decay in the uterus, it becomes more prone to splitting. Undermining both of these observations are the contrary data showing that twins are conceived more frequently in the first three months of marriage, when sexual activity is higher and the mother is younger. Rates rise and fall over time, so that twins were only half as frequent in Sweden in 1960 (before the widespread practice of in vitro fertilization) as they were two centuries before. Seasonal variation may affect twin conceptions; for instance, more twins are conceived in Finland during the long summer days than during the long winter nights, confounding other intuitive notions about human behavior.

One prodigious Texas woman, Sarah Womack, had a set of quintuplets, a set of quadruplets, three sets of triplets, five sets of twins, and nine singletons, producing a total of thirty-seven living children between 1911 and 1933; but the record is held by a nineteenth-century Russian woman who bore sixty-nine children to a peasant named Feydor Vasilet: sixteen twin pairs, seven triplets, four quadruplets, and no single children at all. (Vasilet, incidentally, married a second time and had eighteen children by his second wife in eight pregnancies, his last child was born in 1872 when Vasilet was seventy-five years old.) Since the turn of the century there have been two cases of nonuplets, five octuplets, ten septuplets, and twenty-three sextuplets reported, but few individuals from those births survive—a testament to how perilous multiple birth can be. There are three living sets of sextuplets in the United States (ten in the entire world), fifty quintuplets and more than 400 quadruplets. The largest number of *identical* multiples were the Dionne quintuplets, born in Canada in 1935. Another set of quintuplets, born in Argentina in 1943, consists of a pair of identical twin boys and a set of identical triplet girls.

In the United States about eleven births out of 1,000 are DZ twins, meaning that about one person in fifty has a fraternal twin. The ratio of live multiple births to all live births rose 214 per cent between 1980 and 1994. Triplets increased at seven times the single-birth rate. The number of twin births skyrocketed by thirty-three percent in 1994 alone, the last year for which such figures are available. "The increase is due to two things," says Louis Keith. "One is the aging of the maternal cohort. The number of women over thirty giving birth to children is increasing. These are the women who've gone to school; they're professional women—bankers, lawyers, doctors—who have delayed their first birth. In the United States fully a third of all first births in 1994 went to women over the age of thirty-five. That's only part of the problem. The real increase in twins and triplets in the United States did not occur until 1985, when we learned how to superovulate women. Now doctors are prescribing ovulation-enhancing agents like they were prescribing bubblegum at a children's birthday party."

The same hormones that Yoruba women get from eating yams are used to assist women in ovulating. They are called gonadotrophic hormones, and they affect the timing and release of the monthly eggs. A woman's ovary typically uses only 400 eggs out of the half-million she has available. Hormone derivatives shake the tree. Surplus eggs are released into the fallopian tubes, leading to twin conceptions in about ten percent of the women who take such popular fertility drugs as clomiphene citrate (sold under the names Clomid or Serophene). Pergonal, another powerful drug that helps the egg mature, causes twins in about twenty percent of the pregnancies induced by this method. In vitro fertilization and other relatively new and expensive forms of reproductive technology require taking eggs from the ovary and mixing them with sperm in a petri dish; when the eggs are fertilized, they are placed in the uterus or fallopian tube. Typically more than one fertilized egg is implanted, so the chances of multiple births are quite high.

Although Keith is himself an identical twin, he believes that the worldwide twinning epidemic is a medical emergency. "It's a disaster not only in the United States but in many Western countries. The reason is that multiples mirror the two major problems of modern obstetrics: pre-term delivery and low birth weight. Compared to singletons, twins are ten times more likely to be born prior to the thirty-third week of pregnancy and ten times more likely to be weighing less than 1,500 grams at birth. It's worse for triplets, it's worse for quadruplets, and it's worse for quintuplets. It contributes enormously to the cost for medical care."

While the number of fraternal twins varies across cultures and ethnic groups and families, the rate of identical twinning was thought to be constant—about 3.5 twin births per 1,000—until recently, when the number of identical twins inexplicably began to rise. About one person in every 150 is an identical twin. In the United

States that means that about one-third of all twins are identical, but in Japan, with its low rate of fraternal twinning, nearly two-thirds are identical. This makes statistical estimates between populations rather unreliable. Traditionally, identical twins were distinguished from non-identicals on the basis of sex and appearance: same-sex twins who looked alike were assumed to have been born of the same egg. If the twins were born in the same gestational sac, that was supposed to provide clear proof that they were identical; if they were in separate sacs, they were ruled fraternal, no matter how closely they resembled each other. DNA tests have shown that both of these assumptions are faulty. About a third of identical twins are born from entirely separate placentas, and occasionally the placentas of fraternal twins merge into one. Many same-sex twins who believe that they are fraternal may actually be identical, and vice versa.

7

The Same, but Different

In 1981 an unusual pair of twin girls found their way to the office of John Burn, who was at the Great Ormond Street Hospital for Sick Children in London and is now a professor of genetics at the University of Newcastle-upon-Tyne. Katy and Jenny were friendly, easygoing, eight-year-old girls, who both wore their dark hair in pigtails. Both had distinctive dark, round eyes, slender lips, and long faces that finished in jutting chins. Katy was a gifted gymnast with a lively expression and a bouncy athletic gait. Jenny was notably shorter and weaker. Her calves were swollen, giving a false impression of muscularity; in fact, she had difficulty standing, and she walked with an obvious waddle. Her scores on verbal intelligence tests were also significantly lower than Katy's, reflecting the duller expression in her eyes. Further tests demonstrated what Professor Burn suspected but could scarcely believe: the shorter, weaker, less intelligent twin was suffering from muscular dystrophy; the other twin showed no signs of the disease. And yet according to DNA tests, the twins were identical.

The twins presented, as it were, twin mysteries. Like hemophilia, Fragile X syndrome, and red-green color blindness, muscular dystrophy is carried on the X chromosome and is consequently known as an X-linked disorder. Specifically, it is a flaw in the dystrophene gene, which gives integrity to the muscle membranes and allows them to contract and relax. The particularly savage form of the disease manifested in Jenny, called Duchenne, is a progressive wasting illness that is almost always fatal by the age of twenty. It is usually thought of as a disease that affects only boys.

Females, of course, carry two X chromosomes, whereas males have an X and a Y. When a female zygote discovers that it has twice as many X chromosomes as it requires, an interesting process follows, called X-inactivation: in each cell half of the X chromosomes are turned off. Nature provides a striking way of visualizing this in the form of calico cats, which are exclusively female. Genes for fur colors are carried on the X chromosome: there is one gene for black-and-white coat colors and another gene for the orange-marmalade color. A male cat may be either black and white, or orange, but the female, through X-inactivation, may choose one or the other X chromosome for each pair, producing the calico's patchy coloring.

X-inactivation usually takes place about sixteen days after conception, after twinning is thought to occur. Usually the inactivation is a completely random process; a girl who carries a flaw on her dystrophene gene should have about half of her muscle cells in good working order. Female carriers who do show signs of Duchenne have milder symptoms, and the disease rarely advances. This is because females have the opportunity to select a good gene from their extra X, whereas males are stuck with what their single X offers them. Since few males with muscular dystrophy live long enough to reproduce, the flaw is carried through the maternal line. And yet here was a young girl with all the marks of full-blown Duchenne, which in fact did continue its remorseless progression as Burn and his colleagues studied Jenny over the next several years, placing her in a wheelchair by the age of eleven and leaving her dead at sixteen. Why, Burn wondered, did this girl suffer from a disease that is supposed to be found only in boys? Even stranger, how was it that her identical twin sister was spared this appalling destiny?

John Burn had become interested in twins through his early work on heart defects at Great Ormond Street. "I was struck by the fact that such defects are a remarkably constant problem in time and space, suggesting that they were almost an intrinsic part of being as far as mankind was concerned. At the same time, if you looked in the textbooks, they all said that heart defects are not a genetic problem. Their evidence was based on twins—actually, like those two over there," he said, pointing to a photograph of blond identical twin boys atop his filing cabinet. "One of the twins has a severe heart defect while his brother doesn't. Clearly, said the textbooks, it couldn't possibly be genetic if the twins are identical and they are not both affected." And yet, as a geneticist, Burn noticed that congenital heart defects ran in families; in that respect they certainly behaved like a genetic problem. Moreover, on close examination, the literature on twins revealed a striking excess of heart defects among twins of the same sex, and presumably at least half of them were identical. Was it possible, Burn wondered, that *being* an identical twin caused the defect? "I then spent the next several years collecting lots and lots of twins, both in hospitals and in the community, and the long and short of it is that identical twins are at least twice as likely as singletons to have a heart defect. But typically, like those boys in the picture, it only happens to one of a pair, which implies that the twinning process itself might have caused the trouble."

Soon after that, Burn encountered the twin with muscular dystrophy. When he looked in the scientific literature, he discovered that differences in X-inactivation had shown up in twin girls before. His colleague Elizabeth Tucker at Queen Elizabeth Medical Center in Birmingham had examined a pair of identical twin girls, one above average in intelligence and the other mentally retarded. Although they were physically indistinguishable during their first year of life, their faces had become increasingly different, so that by the age of ten their parents had decided they must be fraternal. Tucker discovered that the retarded twin suffered from Fragile X syndrome, which is caused by breaks in the chromosomal structure. Burn also found that this wasn't the first time that one of a pair of identical twin girls had exhibited signs of muscular dystrophy and the other had not. Because the disease is carried on the X chromosome, Burn reasoned that the discordance between the two girls must have something to do with X-inactivation. "If you took a normal girl and looked at 1,000 cells, you'd expect 500 of those cells to be using mother's X and 500 to be using father's X—just like tossing coins," says Burn. "Now and again, very rarely, a girl will toss heads in every cell, and not tails, and switch off all her good copies." That may have been what happened with Jenny. On the other hand, Burn thought, what if the X-inactivation had occurred *before* the zygote split? Could there be a link between the X-inactivation and the twinning event? "I thought maybe what was happening is that every now and again a ball of cells would end up with a preponderance of mum's X on one side and dad's X on the other. That might actually cause them to separate developmentally. If the two balls of cells are sufficiently different they may say, 'I don't recognize that gang over there—they look different from us. Why don't we make a baby of our own and let them make a baby of their own?' So instead of one girl who is a normal carrier with a mixture of cells, you end up with two girls, one made of cells with the good genes and the other made up of cells with the bad genes." If Burn's theory was correct, then it was the chromosome defect that triggered the twinning, rather than the other way around. Burn thought that if he could understand why Jenny was afflicted and Kate was not, he might find a thread that would unravel the secrets of the twinning process.

As it turned out, Burn was right: the afflicted twin was carrying only her mother's X; her unaffected sister was carrying only her father's X. Could this be characteristic of all identical twin girls? Burn and his colleague Judith Goodship, who was studying X-linked disorders, arranged to collect all the placentas of twin girls born in and around Newcastle over a period of two years. DNA tests of the umbilical cords determined whether the twins were MZ or DZ. Just as Burn had predicted, the survey showed that identical twin girls were more likely to have skewed distribution patterns of the X chromosome. The rest of his theory, however, posited that if one twin had an excess of the mother's X, then the other would mirror her by having an excess of the father's; it was something about that tug-of-war that caused the zygote to break apart in the first place. What he and Goodship found, however, was that if one twin had an excess of mother's X, the other was just as likely to have only father's, or some of mother's and some of father's, or all of mother's—it didn't seem to matter. Therefore the X-inactivation probably took place *after* twinning, not before. However, MZ girls as a group showed more skewing than DZ girls. "Whatever causes identical twinning," says Burn, "these studies show that even though they share the same genes, a genetic trait does not have to be shared. The English language is misleading in calling these twins identical—perhaps we should use the German term *eineiige,* 'one egg.'

"We still need to understand why monozygous twinning is so common in humans and so exceptionally rare in other species," he continues. "I now think that it has something to do with chronology. If you start messing around with the exact timing of ovulation, and fertilization, and implantation, then you might end up creating the conditions that allow twinning to occur. No single magic bullet will explain everything. Some twins will be genetic, some twins will be a case of disturbed development. There might be a fundamental law of physics that the very things that hold cells together will every now and again just come apart. So maybe we shouldn't try to explain everything at once.

"What is fascinating about twins is that they are a condition of humanity which forces all rules to be qualified. Everybody is different—except identical twins. Everybody has got different blood groups—except identical twins. And they are so dramatically visible. They are known to everyone, every writer is aware of the dramatic potential of twins, every kid who ever met identical twins is instantly fascinated by them. They have been known since we have been able to know about anything. Yet we still don't know why they happen. We have all sorts of hypotheses that are given as fact. I now regard a fact as a hypothesis that people don't bother to argue about anymore."

Clearly, some identical twins are more identical than others. "Identical twins are less alike than people think they are," says Nancy L. Segal, a professor of developmental psychology and the director of twin studies at California State University, Fullerton. "Some of the differences are traceable to the early prenatal stages—unequal nutrition, unequal blood supplies. Twins never have completely identical fingerprints. If twins split late there can be differences in mirror-imaging effects—one twin may be right-handed, one left-handed; they may have opposite hair whorls, opposite dental patterns, and opposite birthmarks and moles. While I think identical twins are more alike than any other pair of people you can put together, nevertheless they fall into a relationship vis-à-vis one another, so that one might dominate in certain situations and one might be more submissive. There's a spectrum along which twins differ." Fraternal twins can be so similar that they believe they must be monozygotic, while identicals can be dramatically discordant for facial features, such as cleft lip or palate. An MZ twin who is the product of a placenta that was only marginally attached to the womb may develop into a miniature version of his sibling—as in the premise of the film comedy *Twins,* in which Danny DeVito and Arnold Schwarzenegger play a long-lost identical pair. "None of the correlations that we look at are 1.0," says Segal. "There's differences in virtually everything."

In an examining room at Queen Charlotte's and Chelsea Hospital in London, Dr. Nicholas Fisk placed an ultrasound scanner on the swollen belly of a woman in her nineteenth week of pregnancy. The woman, whom I will call Anita, had been referred to Dr. Fisk because she was carrying twins. The twins were genetically identical, but through some accident inside the womb they had become grotesquely unequal companions. One appeared to be healthy and normal, the other had no head, and its heart contained only a single chamber rather than the usual four. "Obviously, a baby without a proper head doesn't survive," said Fisk, as the monitor read the staticky signal from the scanner. "It is acting as a parasite and getting all the nutrients from the healthy baby, who is our main concern. It is quite difficult for the healthy baby to pump all that blood around to the other twin, which can lead to heart failure."

Anita was considering an experimental procedure that would block the blood flow into the parasitic twin. "This gives us a chance to have one baby perfectly well and healthy," she said. She turned to look at the ultrasound monitor, where the ghostly image of a four-month fetus swam into view. One could see all the way through to its skeletal structure and the vague outlines of its internal organs.

"Here we have the healthy baby," said Fisk, who began taking measurements of its thigh bone on the screen. "Do you feel any bigger, Anita?"

"Slightly."

"It strikes me that it hasn't grown a lot. The heart structure looks completely normal, however," said Fisk as he moved the scanner over the baby's head. "Now here's the baby's face. Can you see that, Anita? You can tell this one is quite healthy because it's moving. Sick babies do not move." He slid the scanner to the right side of Anita's belly, and a totally different creature appeared on the screen. It was a formless mass of tissue with no visible skeleton. The umbilical cord inserted directly into the primitive, single-chambered heart. By using color Doppler Fisk watched the blood flow from the healthy twin into its parasitic sibling.

Anita watched it for a moment, then turned away. You might view it as ironic that I'm a twin," she said. "I'm best friends with my twin brother." She had been hoping for twins. "Maybe we'll still have a chance someday."

Anita's twins suffered from a rare condition called chorioangiopagus parasiticus, or acardia, which is found only in identical twins. It occurs in about one in 30,000 deliveries and usually results in the death of both fetuses. It is an extreme but vivid example of how twins can be genetically identical but biologically different. Most MZ twins share their blood through anastomoses, which are like arteries and veins that run between the twins inside the womb. One sibling usually gains an advantage over the other, with the result that there is typically a greater disparity in size between MZ than DZ twins at birth. Just because twins are "identical" in their genes doesn't mean that they are anatomically the same.

"All of us have got things like moles and skin tags or one finger that's larger than the other," says Judith Hall. "We've all had a mutation in every single gene in our body. Whether it causes a problem depends on what tissue and how early or how late it appears in development. In fact, our bodies are so smart they basically know how to handle mutations and for the most part they just carry on. But if it happens at a very early stage, when cells are growing very rapidly, the self-correcting mechanisms don't seem to be there." Most twins are sufficiently distinct physically that they can easily be distinguished by their parents and close friends. Some identical twins are so different that they don't resemble each other any more than ordinary siblings do.

There have even been at least three instances of genetically identical twins of mixed gender. In each case this confounding event occurred because the female was born with only one X chromosome and no Y (it takes a Y chromosome to make an embryo male). Somehow, possibly because of the twinning process, one twin was stripped of the Y chromosome, and became a female by default—although a special kind of female. These individuals suffer from what is called Turner's syndrome. They are short, broad-chested, with extra folds of skin around the neck, and rudimentary sexual development. The study of Turner's syndrome, which occurs in one out of 10,000 female births, suggests that a second X chromosome is necessary to create normal ovaries and ordinary female growth.

In the strange world of twin studies there is an especially bizarre, but highly influential, case of identical twin boys, one of whom was raised as a girl. Dr. John Money, the distinguished sexologist at Johns Hopkins University in Baltimore, reported the case in his 1972 book (with Anke A. Ehrhardt) *Man and Woman, Boy and Girl.* In October 1963, when the twins were seven months old, the parents took them to a hospital to be circumcised. The doctor used an electrical cauterizing needle rather than a scalpel to perform the procedure. Unfortunately, the doctor applied so much electrical current to the first twin that his entire penis was burned off. A plastic surgeon suggested to the distraught parents that they might consider "reassigning" the sex of the child, on the basis that a vagina is easier to construct than a penis. The parents resisted, but they happened to see a television program about the work being done at Johns Hopkins with transsexuals. "We gave them advice and counseling on the future prognosis and management of their new daughter," wrote Money. The parents changed the name of their "daughter" and began treating her as they would a little girl. Extensive plastic surgery (including castration) and hormonal treatments followed. The daughter was not told that she was a son.

In psychological literature, the child is known as John/Joan. It was Money's belief at the time, which John/Joan reinforced, that gender differences were not inborn, they are created by the environment. "You were born with something that was ready to become your gender identity," he wrote in a later account. "You were wired but not programmed for gender in the same sense that you were wired but not programmed for language. Your gender identity couldn't differentiate as male or female without social stimulation any more than the undifferentiated gonad you started out with could have become testicles or ovaries without the stimulation of your Y or X chromosomes." The varying expectations that family and society place on boys and girls, Money believed, cause them to differentiate into masculine and feminine roles. The twins offered an intriguing opportunity to test this theory.

There is, unfortunately, very little in the literature about the unaffected boy twin, who seems to have developed as a normal heterosexual man. As for John/Joan, Money was able to report that by the age of five, "the little girl already preferred dresses to pants, enjoyed wearing her hair in ribbons, bracelets and frilly blouses, and loved being her daddy's little sweetheart." From birth, John/Joan had always been the dominant twin, but now her dominance expressed itself in a stereotypically feminine manner, and she fussed over her brother "like a mother hen," according to the mother. "Although this girl is not yet a woman," Money wrote in 1975, "her record to date offers convincing evidence that the gender identity gate is open at birth." We are born sexually neutral, in other words, and are pushed by social forces into one camp or the other. "This dramatic case," *Time* magazine reported in 1973, "provides strong support for a major contention of women's liberationists: that conventional patterns of masculine and feminine behavior can be altered. It also casts doubt on the theory that major sex differences, psychological as well as anatomical, are immutably set by the genes at conception."

Was John/Joan an exception to the genetic argument? A rebuttal? How could behavioral geneticists account for such an anomaly? In 1980 BBC television sought to update the story of John/Joan. Money agreed to participate, and then withdrew after psychiatrists working on the case reported that John/Joan was having "considerable ambivalence" over her role as a female.

In 1997 Milton Diamond at the Department of Anatomy and Reproductive Biology, University of Hawaii-Manoa, and H. Keith Sigmundson, a psychiatrist at the Ministry of Health in Victoria, British Columbia, revisited the John/Joan saga. They were aided by the fact that Dr. Sigmundson supervised the therapists involved in the case. They learned that, contrary to the impression Money gave—that Joan was a rather typical little girl—even as a young child she declared that she wasn't a girl. She would rip off dresses her mother tried to put on her, and she refused to mimic putting on makeup and lipstick like her mother; instead, she put on shaving cream and pretended to shave. She knew instinctively that something was wrong. Later, John/Joan recalled: "I looked at myself and said I don't like this type of clothing. I don't like the type of toys I was always being given. I like hanging around with the guys and climbing trees and stuff like that and girls don't like any of that stuff. I looked in the mirror and [saw] my shoulders [were] so wide, I mean there [was] nothing feminine about me . . . that was how I figured it out. [I figured I was a guy] but I didn't want to admit it. I figured I didn't want to wind up opening a can of worms."

Each year, the twins were taken to Johns Hopkins to be examined by the doctors. The children were made to stand naked for inspection by the clinicians and were encouraged to inspect each other—an experience that John/Joan's twin recalls with outrage. At the age of thirteen, Joan ran away from the hospital. She was eventually found hiding on the roof of a nearby building.

When puberty arrived, Joan's problems with peers became unbearable. She was friendless. Girls teased her cruelly, especially when she repeatedly tried to urinate standing up in the girls' bathroom. Sometimes, Joan went to the boys' bathroom. Eventually she was expelled from school when she retaliated against her tormentors forcibly. She became suicidal. Finally she announced her intention to become a boy. Her father then broke down and admitted what had happened fourteen years before. "All of a sudden everything clicked," John/Joan recalls.

The child insisted on receiving male hormone injections. He received a mastectomy, and a phallus was surgically constructed. John soon became accepted as a boy as Joan had never been as a girl. He worked out with weights. At the age of sixteen, he acquired a windowless van with a bed and a bar. "He wanted to lasso some ladies," Diamond told the *New York Times*. Sexual relations were problematic, but possible. John married at twenty-five and adopted his wife's children. According to Diamond, John is happy with life as a man. Certainly his case will no longer be cited as evidence that environment controls sexual identity; indeed, the story of John/Joan will probably be recorded as an example of the forcefulness of nature, which powerfully exerts itself even when good intentions conspire to deceive it.

There may be an important difference between identical twins who separated early in embryogenesis (and therefore came to term in separate placentas) and those who separated later. "There is evidence now from four studies that placentation does make a difference in twin resemblance," says Richard Rose, a psychologist at Indiana University in Bloomington. "There's no *genetic* variation—they're all monozygotic—but the early separating twins are significantly less alike for many dimensions of personality. Neither I nor anyone else knows quite what that represents. It could be a consequence of differences in the in utero environment, or it simply could be a consequence of the actual timing of the embryological splitting in the twinning process. We certainly do know that genetic differences are not the cause of these behavior differences, because they're all genetic replicas."

The most dramatic examples of late-separating twins, of course, are conjoined twins, who are notorious for their conflicting personalities. Chang and Eng Bunker occasioned the term Siamese twins because of their birth in 1811 in Siam (modern Thailand). Joined at the abdomen, the Bunker brothers toured the United States with the P. T. Barnum circus, eventually becoming quite wealthy and retiring to a farm in North Carolina. There they married two sisters and succeeded in fathering twenty-two children, none of whom were twins. Chang had a reputation for an explosive temper, and he became an alcoholic when his health began to fail. Eng, the calmer brother, was a lifelong teetotaler. He was so alarmed by his brother's drinking that he sought to be surgically separated, but no doctor would attempt the operation. Masha and Dasha, a pair of Russian twins born during the Second World War, have a single lower body and an upper body that is entirely separate. They spent their childhood in vigorous, sometimes violent disagreements, warring over their differing tastes in music, television, and exercise. Abigail and Brittany Hensel, who were born in 1990, are unusual even among conjoined twins, having only two legs and an undivided torso (only four such sets have been recorded). Although one is a hearty eater, and the other picks at her food, so far they don't seem to have developed the oppositional personalities that have characterized other well-known conjoined sets.

About twenty-five percent of identical twins show features of mirror imaging, a reversal of laterality that is most commonly detected when twins have opposite-handedness. In its mildest form, mirror imaging can be a matter of which side of the mouth the first tooth appears on, but it can also be more dramatic, as in twins whose organs are actually found on the wrong side of their bodies. This condition appears frequently in conjoined twins, a circumstance that has led most researchers to conclude that mirror imaging is characteristic of late-separating MZ twins only. It became an article of faith that twins who had opposite-handedness must be identical, even when there were obvious differences in eye and hair color. "It turns out that there is no difference between identical and fraternal twins in the frequency of left-handedness," says Charles Boklage. "The mirror image thing is a cute idea that came from the 1920s, before there was blood typing. Now, there is such a thing as mirror imaging. My own twin daughters—I used to think that they were monozygotic twins. I found out not long ago they're not. They always looked practically identical, but there were impressionistic differences. One day I discovered why. I held a child up in front of the mirror. Now, I'm used to seeing my face in a mirror, but I wasn't used to seeing hers. What it did was reverse the asymmetries in her face." Her face metamorphosed into the image of her sister. Boklage contends that mirror imaging is just as frequent in DZ twins, such as his daughters, as it is with MZs.

Twins of both kinds have a higher rate of left-handedness, and some scientists, such as Luigi Gedda, the director of the Mendel Institute in Rome, have suggested that left-handed singletons may be survivors of a vanished-twin pair. Like twins, lefties are a puzzling minority whose origins have never been satisfactorily explained. Their brains develop differently from right-handers; for instance, right-handers tend to rely on the left hemisphere of their brain for language, whereas left-handers are more diffuse in their neurological organization. They are more likely to be alcoholics, psychotics, epileptics, dyslexics, and to suffer from allergies and autoimmune disorders. Some evidence suggests they tend to be gifted and precocious, especially in mathematics. The higher rate of non-right-handedness among twins is often accounted for as "birth stress," but that wouldn't explain why there are more lefties among their non-twin relatives. Nancy Segal thinks that left-handedness may have two causes, birth trauma and late separation, that give rise to separate problems or talents. Boklage believes that because non-right-handedness (a term he uses to include ambidexterity) is found at a higher rate in twins of both types and their family members, there must be a highly heritable factor that both forms of twinning have in common.

Few studies have examined the phenomenon of mirror imaging, and those that do have largely failed to show a significant difference between opposite-handed pairs. Boklage, however, decided to examine the data for schizophrenia in identical twins, a major battlefield in the war against environmentalists. If you are a twin who has schizophrenia, the chances that your identical sibling has it as well are about thirty to fifty percent, according to various studies. For a fraternal twin, the odds fall to about ten percent—about the same as for a non-twin sibling. Obviously, there is a genetic contribution, even if it is modest. But if schizophrenia is inherited, why don't both twins suffer from it simultaneously? Perhaps there are certain environmental triggers that set off the disease in a vulnerable individual, for instance, one twin might experience a trauma or a stressful event that the other does not. The problem with this appealing theory is that nothing in the environment has ever been demonstrated to cause schizophrenia. Boklage noticed that if one looked only at right-handed twins who are schizophrenic, the chances of an identical sibling suffering from schizophrenia jumped to ninety-two percent. When one member of a twin pair is schizophrenic and the other is not, one or both of them is left-handed. Moreover, left-handed schizophrenics tended to be less severely ill than the right-handers.

In 1990 the Keith twins (along with Alexander Golbin, an assistant professor of psychiatry at the University of Illinois, and Irene Golbin, his research assistant) surveyed twenty-seven mirror-image MZ twins, fifty-three non-mirror-image twins, and twenty-four DZ twins (four of whom showed mirroring) at the annual Twins Day Festival in Twinsburg, Ohio. The researchers were particularly interested in finding certain sleep irregularities, such as bedwetting, teeth grinding, apnea, insomnia, sleepwalking, and nightmares. They discovered startling differences among the mirror-image "identicals," who seemed to be quite polarized in their sleeping habits, compared with the non-mirroring MZ and the DZ group. The researchers postulated that there may be a psychological mirroring that goes along with the physical, each reflecting a profound biological polarization. It could possibly explain opposing tendencies in personality, sex orientation, and susceptibility to disease.

Behavior geneticists have spent the last thirty years waging war against the environmentalist belief that people are fundamentally alike, and are made different only by their families, their schooling, the traumas of life—by their environments, in other words. Now, after decades of persuasive twin studies showing how similar identical twins are to each other, even when they have been raised in separate families, behavior geneticists must face the question of why identical twins should differ at *all.* They have the same genes, and studies have shown again and again that the influence of common family background on intelligence, personality, and behavior is modest to negligible for most measurable traits. And yet identical twins do differ from each other, often quite stunningly. For instance, several studies have shown that an identical twin who is homosexual stands a fifty percent chance of having a gay twin. But if homosexuality is genetically determined, why wouldn't the chances be closer to one hundred percent? Does the environment play a role after all? And if so, how? What is it in the environment that affects us and makes us different from each other, and different, in some respects, from ourselves, the selves we might have been if genes alone control who we are? The differences in identical twins may turn out to be more informative than their similarities.

8

The Emotional Life

One of the most provocative questions in the nature-versus-nurture debate concerns the influence of genes on criminal behavior. Twin studies in Nazi Germany confidently placed the heritability of criminality at 60 or 70 percent. Although more recent American studies tell us that there is a genetic connection to the antisocial behavior of very young children, they also point out that from adolescence on the environment plays an increasingly important role. In Sweden, where all adoptions are recorded for national statistics, a 1982 study found that the rate of criminality in adopted children was 2.9 percent when neither their biological nor adoptive parents had committed a crime; the figure rose to 6.7 percent if their adoptive parents were criminal and 12.1 percent if their biological parents were criminal. That would seem to be a nice demonstration of the relative weight of environment and genetics on antisocial behavior. If *both* sets of parents were criminal, however, the chances of the child being criminal as well were 40 percent. Together, genes and environment appear to be several times more compelling than either force acting alone.

Cancer also shows the effects of genes and environment acting in concert. For ten years Thomas Mack, a professor of preventive medicine at the University of Southern California, has been building a registry of adult twins with chronic diseases, and he has now identified more than 17,000 twins with cancer, Hodgkin's disease, multiple sclerosis, and autoimmune disease. According to Mack's data, a twin whose identical co-twin has Hodgkin's is one hundred times more likely to get the disease than a fraternal twin whose sibling has the disease, which demonstrates how powerfully genetic Hodgkin's is. On the other hand, out of the 500 twins he studied in which melanomas had occurred, there were only ten instances of both twins having the disease, indicating that despite the genetic contribution of inherited traits such as light skin, a powerful environmental influence is at work. If you are an identical twin with breast cancer, which is known to be a familial disease, the chances that your co-twin will also get the disease is about five times as high as the average; still, not all co-twins get the disease. The likelihood of getting breast cancer is affected by the age of first menstruation: the younger a woman is when she has her first period, the higher her chances of developing breast cancer in the future. Breast cancer rates also rise with a woman's age at first pregnancy and with her age at menopause. In each case, environmental factors create differences between identical twins, and those differences affect the health of women who are equally susceptible to disease.

Perhaps the most puzzling feature of identical twins is their love life. They do have much in common. David Lykken and his colleague Matt McGue examined 1,500 sets of twins from the Minnesota Twin Registry, finding that if one identical twin had been divorced, there was a forty-five percent chance that the other twin would also have been divorced, a rate that is twenty-five percent above the average for Minnesotans. Lykken postulates that genes influence divorce rates through personality characteristics that contribute to or detract from marital harmony. Identical twins tend to have their first date at about the same time and to date with equal frequency. They begin sexual activity at about the same time, and the intensity of their sexual drive, as well as their sexual dysfunctions, tends to be very similar. They marry and begin having children at roughly the same points in their lives, although there doesn't seem to be much correlation between the number of children each twin has. The extraordinary difference between identical twins lies in whom they choose to marry.

When Louis Keith was in medical school in Chicago, he had a friend named Phyllis Markuson. They dated a couple of times but were never more than pals. On New Year's Eve of 1960, Phyllis bumped into Louis's identical twin, Donald, at the ballet. Louis and Donald were as physically alike as identical twins can be, both of them dark-eyed, long-lashed, full-lipped, Latin-lover types. Donald, who was just home from the army on leave, was wearing his dress blues. "There was just something different about him, like a spark," Phyllis recalls. "They were both very good-looking. I think Louis has softer features, especially around the mouth. Donald is more angular. His jaw is more set and refined, which reflects his personality. But who knows what one sees in another person—physically, emotionally, or intellectually—that makes him different from everybody else." Phyllis was instantly smitten, and so was Donald.

Immediately after the meeting, he called his brother and asked if he had any romantic intentions where Phyllis was concerned. "Most twins know this area is a big, fat, hot potato," says Donald. Louis told him he liked Phyllis, but he wasn't romantically interested.

"Are you sure?" asked Donald. "I don't want you to say ten years from now that I stole a girl you were interested in." Donald and Phyllis went out every night for forty-four nights in a row. "I had a thirty-day leave and I got a fifteen-day extension," says Donald. They have now been married for thirty-two years. "It's lucky we don't have the same taste in women," says Donald. "It would be very difficult going through life wanting the same spouse."

Although there have been many instances of twins competing for the same potential partner, the relationship between Phyllis and the Keith twins is more typical. In 1993 Lykken and Auge Tellegen, also a psychologist at the University of Minnesota, reported on a study of about 1,000 middle-aged twins and their spouses, which examines various widely held assumptions about mate selection. One is that we tend to choose mates who are similar to ourselves. When Lykken and Tellegen compared sets of twins with the people they had chosen to marry, they discovered that, in fact, traditionalism, physical attractiveness, education, and height were strongly correlated, but in other respects spouses had too little in common to explain their selection of each other. A second assumption is that we are all looking for a special someone who has certain qualities that we admire. Presumably identical twins who have been raised together will have similar criteria; after all, they do tend to make very similar choices about clothes and furniture and holidays. But, when Lykken and Tellegen compared the spouses of identical twins, they resembled each other even less than they resembled the twin they were married to; they were no more alike than people who were married to unrelated individuals. Another surprise was the fact that when the twins were asked to evaluate their twin's spouse, about as many disliked the spouse as not. The spouses, for their part, returned the favor, although one would expect that the spouses would be at least somewhat attracted to the identical twin. And, while nearly twice as many husbands of identical twins approved of the other twin as did the wives of identical twins, even among the husbands a quarter were not attracted at all to the identical twin and only thirteen percent agreed that they "could have fallen for her myself." Among wives, the figure was only seven percent.

"We are left with a curious and disquieting conclusion," Lykken and Tellegen wrote.

> Although most human choice behavior lawfully reflects the characteristics of the chooser and of the choice, the most important choice of all, that of a mate, seems to be an exception. Although we do tend to choose from among people like ourselves, another person who is remarkably like ourselves (our MZ twin) is not likely to be drawn to the same choice we make. Having made a choice, when we are then confronted with a second mate candidate who is remarkably like the person we have chosen, we are not also strongly attracted to that person.

The authors concluded that human pairing is inherently random: "Romantic infatuation, we suggest, like imprinting, forms an initial bond almost adventitiously and then sustains it long enough, in most instances, for an enduring bond to be forged by the slower processes of learning and adaptation that result in compassionate love."

Several other twin studies have begun to look at what makes people happy. The findings so far point to two independent components of happiness, one called extraversion, or positive emotionality, and the other called neuroticism, or negative emotionality. Curiously, the two traits appear to operate independently of each other, and not, as might be expected, like a seesaw, where a rise of one marks a decline of the other. A person who is free of negative moods is not necessarily happy, just as a person who never experiences positive moods is not necessarily unhappy. Some researchers have proposed that both extroversion and neuroticism arise out of particular situations, with positive experiences leading to positive emotionality, and negative experiences to negative emotionality. This is the basic environmentalist stance: that an accumulation of pleasant experiences will endow a person with a happy nature, while unpleasant experiences have the opposite effect. Other researchers assert that both extroversion and neuroticism are genetically disposed.

To test these theories, Laura Baker, a professor of psychology at the University of Southern California who heads the Southern California Twin Project, recruited some fifty sets of twins from the Los Angeles area, who ranged in age from sixteen to seventy-two. The twin study was done in conjunction with a family study comprising three generations of 220 families. What the study found was that the more closely family members were related, the more similar they were in experiencing negative emotionality; that is, levels of this trait were more alike among fraternal twins and siblings, who share, on average, fifty percent of their genes, than among grandparents and grandchildren, who have about a quarter of their genes in common. This finding suggests the presence of a marked genetic effect where neuroticism is concerned. Predictably, MZ twins were much more alike in this respect than DZ twins. But a different conclusion emerged when positive emotionality was measured. The differences between MZ twins and DZ twins were not nearly so great; suggesting that shared experiences, instead of genetics, may influence levels of positive emotionality.

Unhappy natures, as we might as well call the negative element of happiness, seemed to pass through the generations in genes of descendants. Yet happiness itself seems to be largely a gift of the environment—in particular, the family environment. Although countless studies have now documented the paucity of the effect that ordinary families have on children, Baker's study suggests that the one thing a good family can do is to make a child happy.

9

The Environment We Make

SHOULD COUPLES BE required to obtain a license before they are allowed to become parents? This notion has been proposed by David Lykken. "We already have criteria for parents who adopt a child," Lykken said as he sat in his office at the University of Minnesota amid piles of books and research papers. "Typically, the parents have to be mature." There has to be a father and a mother, and they have to have means of support, and they can't be actively psychotic or seriously criminal. I say that our problems are not going to be mitigated until we establish similar criteria for those who would produce children biologically.

"I think if you put children with a sociopathic, immature, irresponsible, drug-addicted teenage mother, there's a high-percentage chance that the child is also going to be a sociopath," he continued. "We know that mothers of illegitimate children are [on average] ten points lower in IQ than mothers of legitimate children. So one of the interesting consequences, if we do something to stem the tide of illegitimacy, would be to reduce the number of low IQ children." In Lykken's scheme, an "unlicensed woman" who got pregnant, and who wanted to carry her baby to term, would be placed in a maternity home, so that the developing child would not be harmed by drugs or alcohol. "As soon as the child is born, he is taken away and put in a foster home and put up for adoption," Lykken explains. After a second violation, the unlicensed mother would have to submit to a surgical implantation of a time-release birth-control drug called Norplant, which chemically sterilizes the woman for up to five years. Fathers would be tracked down and identified through DNA testing and made to pay a portion of their future salaries to support the children they helped to create.

Lykken's plan is a grandchild of Sir Francis Galton's nineteenth-century idea of parenting quotas, intended to cull the undesirables from Britain's genetic stock. Although even Lykken considers it unlikely that his licensing plan will become law anytime soon, it is social engineering like that that causes people to be terrified of behavior genetics. "A lot of social scientists are so scandalized by my proposals that they think I must be a Fascist," Lykken says. "But I consider myself to be a political atheist." Lykken is a well-respected researcher who is known for taking authoritarian positions on public policy. He has recently published a new book, *The Antisocial Personalities,* in which he contends that what turns children into sociopaths is not genes but the environment—particularly an environment of a fatherless home and an illiterate mother. "It has become part of the received knowledge from twin studies in recent years that being reared together in the same home does not make siblings more alike, and that puzzles people. The one real exception to that is socialization—learning how to avoid breaking the rules that are necessary for living together," says Lykken. "We know that criminality runs in families. Thirty percent of arrestees have a brother already in the slammer. There's no question that a small group of chronic criminals who are responsible for sixty percent or more of crime in this country tend to come from the same areas, the same social classes, the same families. When you look at the home in which the typical juvenile delinquent grows up, you don't need a study in order to be convinced that this is a pathogenic environment. It's mind-boggling the kinds of homes in which several million American adolescents are currently developing into little sociopaths."

Lykken acknowledges that most of the unlicensed parents who would be penalized under his proposed measure would be black, since he says that illegitimacy is some six times higher among blacks than whites. "I think that is the explanation for the difference between black and white crime," says Lykken. "One-eighth of the population is responsible for one-half of the violent crime, but I think that is because such a high proportion of black males are reared without fathers. So if we could accomplish by some magic a reduction to a very low level of illegitimacy in both races, I think crime rates would plummet and would equalize between the races, and even the IQ differences would be smaller than they are. This is important to me because one of my three sons married an African-American lady and I have three African-American grandchildren."

Race and IQ have haunted the study of human genetics, because historically the IQ scores of blacks have consistently been lower on average than those of whites. At the center of the IQ controversy is Sandra Scarr, a former colleague of Lykken and Bouchard at the University of Minnesota who is now a professor of psychology at the University of Virginia. (She is also the past president of the Behavior Genetics Association and the American Psychological Society.) Scarr was one of the first researchers to conduct twin studies in minority racial populations. Brilliant and dauntingly prolific, much praised and often damned, Scarr has divided the academy because she has insisted on applying the insights of behavioral genetics to developmental psychology.

Early in her career, Scarr began studying why so many black children did poorly on tests and in school achievement. She wondered whether it was the result of sociocultural disadvantage or genetically based racial differences. "I thought that there were only a few ways to ask that question," she recalls. "There was no point in documenting yet again that on average blacks score lower than whites. Just documenting that black children did poorly on tests, we already knew that. So I turned to testing black twins in order to look at the genetic and environmental variation within the black community."

It was a taboo question in the early seventies, when Scarr began testing black twins in the Philadelphia schools. Arthur Jensen's 1969 article "How Much Can We Boost IQ?" had stirred up a nasty debate by airing his theory that whites are genetically superior to blacks in intelligence. Two years later, Richard Herrnstein's article on IQ in the *Atlantic* rekindled the same debate. After watching the public pillorying of Jensen and Herrnstein when their articles appeared, Scarr decided that if her data supported a substantial relationship between African ancestry and low intellectual skills, she would have to leave the country. In fact, it didn't, and she remained, to become one of the most acclaimed and controversial of American psychologists.

One of the most striking findings from Scarr's early twin work was that, while studies had shown a closer correlation between the IQ scores of white identical twins than between those of white fraternals, the scores of both identical *and* fraternal black twins were similar. A set of black fraternal twins was less likely to diverge widely in intelligence; there was less likely to be one clever and one slow twin. Scarr speculated that the differences were suppressed by the depredations of the black child's environment. When she compared the IQ scores for white children at the bottom of the socioeconomic ladder, it turned out that environmental differences were just as controlling for them. Scarr's findings suggested that inner-city black children—and white children in the same severely deprived circumstances—could have the genes for a higher intelligence than their environment permitted them to express. In 1972, soon after Scarr began teaching at the University of Minnesota (a move that seems almost inevitable for anyone interested in twin studies), she and one of her students, Andrew Pakstis, decided to test Jensen's theory that intelligence differences between whites and blacks were genetic in origin. Scarr and Pakstis reasoned that if Jensen was right, children of mixed black and white parentage (which is true of most African Americans) would score higher on IQ tests according to their proportion of white ancestry. But subsequent tests of Philadelphia twins found no relation between intellectual-performance scores and the degree of white genetic background.

Then Scarr, along with Richard A. Weinberg, a psychologist who worked with her at Minnesota's Institute of Child Development, decided to conduct an adoption study, which is another way of deciphering the relative contribution of genes and the environment on the formation of human intelligence and personality. Adoption studies are a natural complement to twin studies, since the one investigates genetically unrelated people raised in the same environment, and the other examines genetically identical people raised in the same or (in the case of separated twins) different environments.

Scarr and Weinberg looked at 130 black and mixed-race children, ranging in age from four to twelve, who had been adopted by well-off white families. The average IQ of these children was 106, which was higher than the mean of 100 for the general population and well above the average score of 90 for black children in the region. The earlier the children had been adopted, the better they fared. Scarr and Weinberg estimated that the scores of these early-adopted children could be about twenty points higher than those of comparable children reared in the black community. It seemed clear that the environment influenced IQ considerably. Being reared in the culture of the tests and the schools apparently made a large difference in achievement.

At the same time, however, Scarr and Weinberg were studying a group of white adolescents, ages sixteen to twenty-two, who had been adopted in early infancy and were at the end of their childhood. The adopting families were all white, across the middle range of the socioeconomic spectrum.* "We were interested in seeing the cumulative effects of the family-rearing environment on IQ scores," says Scarr. "We were astonished at the results." The hypothesis of the study was that if the family environment mattered, then at the end of the child-rearing period adopted children would show the maximum effects of the advantages and disadvantages of the families that had taken them in. The IQ scores of the adolescents were about the same as the black and interracial children in the other study. The disconcerting revelation from the adolescent study was that after adopted children and natural children were reared to-

*One weakness of adoption studies is that they underrepresent families living in poverty, since such families are rarely permitted to adopt children. Therefore, inferences about the environment can only be drawn from the broadly constituted middle class.

gether for eighteen years, the IQ scores of the adopted children bore *no relation at all* to those of the natural children in the same family or to those of their adopted parents.* "We had expected children reared in the same family to resemble each other *more* in IQ and personality than the young children in our transracial study, but we were dead wrong on both counts." The young black adopted children in the other study were more similar to their white siblings than the adopted adolescents in the new study were to their siblings, despite the fact that the adolescents had spent their entire childhood with their adopted families and were of the same race. "This was really interesting," says Scarr. "First we were amazed in the adolescent-adoption study that we did not find any resemblances among people unless they were genetic relatives. This did not jibe with previous adoption literature or with our own transracial adoption study. We tried to figure out why adolescents bore so little resemblance to their adoptive families."

Scarr found that children in the same family who were genetically unrelated were alike in early years but grew to be different over time. They became more like their biological parents, whom they didn't know, than like the adoptive parents who raised them, not only in social attitudes, vocational interests, and unexpected personality features, such as prejudice and rigidity of belief, but also in IQ. A follow-up study of the black and mixed-race children who were adopted into white homes found that by adolescence their IQ scores had fallen to a point slightly above what would be the average for their racial and ethnic mixture in the area. It was similar to the progression

*A well-known Texas adoption study found similar results: moderate IQ correlation between genetically unrelated siblings in childhood dropping to essentially zero by late adolescence—and what is more, they were the *same children* measured at two ages (ten years apart).

of mental development observed between MZ and DZ twins: the two types start out life being almost equally alike but diverge as they pass through childhood, the MZ twins becoming even more similar and the DZ twins going their separate ways.

One lesson from the adopted-adolescent study seemed to be that genetic differences cause individuals to respond differently to similar rearing conditions. Another interesting revelation was that adopted children raised in rural or working-class homes did not differ significantly from adopted children raised by professional parents. From these two findings, Scarr concluded that black and white children were essentially alike in their inherent intelligence or their ability to achieve in school, provided that they were given realistic opportunities to become a part of the culture of the tests and of the schools. Social-class differences among whites, however, were largely attributable to genetic differences. As long as children in a population are reasonably nurtured, Scarr observed, the individual differences between them must be genetic. Therefore, efforts to improve intellectual or academic performance should concentrate on rescuing those who were living on the far margins of society, who were genuinely deprived and unable to gain the skills or knowledge needed to compete in the mainstream culture.

Over the last fifteen years, Scarr has been refining a new theory of development, based largely on her conviction that environments do influence the intellects of young children. At early stages of life, she observed, enriched environments, such as day-care centers with stimulating programs, can boost a deprived child's achievement. So environments can make a difference in the intellects of young children. Even young children, however, are genetically programmed to create certain experiences for themselves. For instance, a smiling, gregarious baby is more likely to be cuddled and petted than a fussy and undemonstrative one. If these two dissimilar infants are siblings, their experiences of living in the same home can be quite different. As children mature, they gain more and more control over their environment and actively select from the superabundance of opportunities those that conform to their genetic disposition. The distinction between genes and environment becomes less and less clear. "The dichotomy of nature and nurture has always been a bad one, not only for the oft-cited reasons that both are required for development, but because a false parallel arises between the two," Scarr wrote (in collaboration with her student Kathleen McCartney) in the 1983 journal *Child Development.* "We propose that development is indeed the result of nature and nurture, but that genes drive experience. Genes are components in a system that organizes the organism to experience the world."

That would explain why MZ twins become more similar over time and DZ twins less so. Identical genes compel MZ twins to experience the world in a similar manner, thus reinforcing the similarities of their natures; whereas the genetic variation of DZ twins awakens different interests and talents, which inevitably pull the twins apart into more distinct individuals. Identical twins who have been reared separately may live in different families, even in different cultures, but they evoke similar responses from their environment and are disposed by their natures to make similar choices and to build similar niches for themselves.

In this school of thought, environment and genes are not separate, countervailing forces. It may not even make sense to parcel out traits, such as IQ or features of personality, into percentages of heritability versus environment, because after one reaches a certain age the environment is itself a heritable reflection of one's genetic disposition. We make our environments, rather than the other way around; that is, as long as the environment we find ourselves in is not so deprived or abusive that normal development cannot occur. "Good enough" parents, who provide an average environment to support development, will have the same effects on their children as "superparents" who press upon their children every cultural advantage. "In this view," Scarr argues, "human experience is the construction of reality, not a property of a physical world that imparts the same experience to everyone who encounters it."

Consider the example of major depression in women, which is known to run in families, but which intuitively seems to be a response to personal conflicts, emotional traumas, or past family problems: environmental influences, in other words. A study by Kenneth S. Kendler, a psychiatrist, and his colleagues at the Medical College of Virginia examined more than 1,000 female twins, both fraternal and identical. As expected, identical twins were more alike in their susceptibility to depression than fraternal twins, but the genetic factor was not overwhelming. The scientists calculated the heritability of major depression ranged between thirty-three and forty-five percent: it was strongly influenced by genetic factors, in other words, but not preponderantly so. Similar rates of heritability have been found for heart disease, stroke, and peptic ulcers, and far higher rates for schizophrenia, hypertension, and bipolar illness. In the case of depression, environmental experiences are more clearly controlling than genes.

But what kind of experiences?

Behavioral geneticists break down the vast term "environment" into two parts, shared and non-shared. The shared environment is what twins or other siblings have in common—specifically, their family, neighborhood, church, social status, the child-raising techniques of their parents—the home matrix that they grow up in. The non-shared environment is whatever those siblings do on their own. If one takes maths and the other poetry, those are non-shared experiences, even though they may attend the same school. If one breaks an arm playing baseball and the other falls in love with a cheerleader, those are non-shared experiences, despite the commonalities of childhood accidents and teenage romances. Even certain biological differences, such as might be caused by birth trauma and hormonal imbalances in the womb, would be marked as features of non-shared environments between identical twins. Between other siblings, differences in sex, age, birth order, and treatment by the parents would all be non-shared environments.

Kendler and his colleagues discovered that the kind of shared environments one would intuitively expect to lead to depression in later life—such as the early loss of a parent, the social class one was reared in, the parental child-rearing practices—plays at best only a very modest role. This confirmed findings by Bouchard's separated-twins studies that the contribution of the common family environment to the development of personality is virtually nil, and Scarr's adoption studies that the family accounts for about five percent of measurable personality traits. It is the non-shared environment that causes depression. The distinction is important because the non-shared environment is the life we lead on our own. It is what happens to us as individuals. It is the life we choose for ourselves, not the life our parents make for us.

"The statement that parents have few differential effects on children does not mean that not having parents is just as good as having parents. It may not matter much that children have *different* parents, but it does matter that they have parent(s) or some supportive, affectionate person who is willing to be parent-like," Scarr said, in a 1991 presidential address to the Society for Research in Child Development. "To see the effects of having no parents (or parent surrogates), one would have to return to the orphanages of long ago . . . or see children trapped in crack houses of inner cities in the United States, locked in basements and attics by vengeful, crazy relatives. Really deprived, abusive, and neglectful environments do not support normal development for any child." Despite these distinctions, Scarr's speech was attacked by some developmental psychologists and others who fought her election and bitterly oppose her views, believing that they discourage efforts to improve the welfare of children—especially black children—and fail to hold parents accountable for their children's behavior. In fairness, Scarr concedes that parents can have effects on children's motivation and self-esteem, but she insists that, beyond a minimum level of nurturing, they have little measurable impact on intelligence, interests, and personality.

10

Beyond Nature versus Nurture

Twins threaten us because they undermine our notion of identity. We think we are who we are because of the life we have lived. We think we shape the character and values of our children by the way we raise them. We think that we are born with the potential to be many things, and to behave in an infinite variety of ways, and that we consciously navigate a path through the obstacles and opportunities that life presents us with, through a faculty we call free will. But when we read about twins who have been separated at birth and reunited in middle age only to discover that in many respects they have become the same person, it suggests that life is a charade, that the experiences that we presume have shaped us are little more than ornaments or curiosities we have picked up along the way, and that the injunctions of our parents or the traumas of our youth that we believed to have been the lodestones of our character may have had little more effect on us than a book we may have read or a show we may have seen on television. The science of behavioral genetics, largely through twin studies, has made a persuasive case that much of our identity is stamped on us from conception; to that extent our lives seem to be pre-chosen—all we have to do is live out the script that is written in our genes.

But this view, for most people, seems stark and frightening and full of dire political and philosophical consequences. If we are only living out our lives like actors reading our lines, then the nobility of life is cheapened. Our accomplishments are not really earned, they are simply arrived at. Our failures are just as expectable. We are like genetic rockets, programmed to travel in a set direction with a given amount of fuel. Barring some accident of fate, our trajectory is predetermined—we're just along for the ride.

Moreover, if some of us are more inclined toward sin—however it may be defined—because we are genetically more violent, more lustful, more greedy, or less religious, then theology has new questions to ask itself. Are some people "chosen" because they are born meek and devout? What does free will mean if nature has already shortened the spectrum of opportunity within ourselves?

Since Galton's first twin study more than a hundred years ago, there has been a nonstop debate over the relative contributions of genes and environment to the creation of intelligence. The question of what constitutes intelligence has dogged the debate from the start. Galton himself developed a primitive test of mental abilities, based on the speed and sensitivity of sensory perceptions. In the early part of the twentieth century, Alfred Binet, a psychologist at the Sorbonne, constructed a series of tests designed to measure a person's ability to identify patterns, draw analogies, and solve problems. He assigned each of the various tasks involved in the test a "mental age," which was the youngest age a child of normal intelligence could be expected to accomplish the task successfully. When the mental age was divided by the chronological age, the concept of the "intelligence quotient" was born.

By testing twins and other family members, it was possible to demonstrate that IQ levels were heritable. *How* heritable became one of the great debates of the new century. The eugenics movement, which was to some extent the child of IQ testing, made the assumption that genes were almost entirely responsible for intelligence and that environmental influences were negligible. By the 1960s it was clear that such an assumption was unsubstantiated by the data; moreover, the world had suffered the hideous consequences of the unbridled hereditarian viewpoint. The study of human genetics was colored by American racism, British classism, and Nazi ethnic madness. As eugenics fell into disrepute, extremists in the environmental school began to trumpet their own bias, which was that nearly all of our intelligence is the result of conditioning and that genes play little, if any, role.

This argument also failed, in part because of the emergence of more rigorous and intensive studies of identical twins raised apart. These studies generally placed the heritability of intelligence at about 0.75; however, other kinship and adoption studies, as well as different models of evaluating the data, arrive at lower figures, between 0.40 and 0.60. A 1990 analysis of various kinship studies calculated the heritability of IQ to be 0.51. However, in other studies the heritability of IQ appeared to increase as the twins grew older, which would make the figure derived from studies of twins reared apart more plausible. Shared environmental effects, on the other hand, appear to account for twenty to thirty percent of the variance in IQ, with unshared environment accounting for a larger portion. Some prominent critics of the hereditarian view have proposed that the reason twins are more alike than ordinary siblings in intelligence is that they shared the same environment in the womb. Even if this proves to be true, the shared environment they are speaking of ends at birth. We are still left with the question of what in the environment affects us after we are born. Adoption studies have repeatedly demonstrated very little shared environmental influence on cognitive ability—about thirty percent in studies of children or adolescents, but declining to four percent when adopted children are studied as adults. The battle over these percentage points has been ferocious, and to a disinterested observer it can seem almost comical. The unstated goal of each side of the debate seems to be to lay claim to more than fifty percent of intelligence—thus one side wins and the other loses.

In the last twenty years, the argument over nature versus nurture has spread to encompass every aspect of human development. Personality was a late entrant in this contest, largely because no one knew exactly what qualities to measure, or how. That changed with the development of a number of different personality inventories and the recruitment of an enormous population of twins to the many twin registries around the world. Behavioral geneticists divide up personality traits in various ways, but one of the most widely accepted paradigms has been put forward by Hans Eysenck at the Institute of Psychiatry in London. Eysenck proposed that the personality could be described along three axes, which he labeled Extraversion, Neuroticism, and Psychoticism. Each of these dimensions encompasses many common traits. The realm of Extraversion, for instance, sets the outgoing, impulsive, lively personality at one end of the spectrum and the shy introvert at the other. The Neuroticism axis runs from the well-adjusted, stable personality to the anxious, guilty, emotionally unstable personality. Psychoticism includes gradients of criminality and mental disorders, but also such traits as creativity. Using twin data, Bouchard and others have placed the overall heritability of personality at about fifty percent—somewhat less than the claims that the geneticists lay to intelligence, but still quite high.

If genes account for half the development of the personality, then environment must account for the remainder. Using increasingly sophisticated models to analyze the data, behavioral geneticists were able to ask a new and highly pertinent question: what, exactly, in the environment shapes personality? Their answer is that the common shared environment—the family, the neighborhood, the parents' income and level of education, their way of raising children—has essentially no effect on the development of personality. Identical twins who have been reared apart are not much different in various personality measurements than twins reared together. This is arguably the most surprising and important discovery of the entire field of behavioral genetics. It is the individual experiences that each person has, such as the education he receives, the friends he makes, birth order, accidents—the unshared environment—that account for nearly all the personality difference that can be ascribed to nongenetic factors.

Heritabilities of social attitudes are even higher than for personality: 0.65 for radicalism, for instance, 0.54 for toughmindedness, and 0.59 for religious leisure time interests (the amount of time a person might spend in church or reading religious texts). In fact, identical twins reared apart were actually somewhat more alike in their attitudes than identical twins reared together. Various tests of ability show extremely high levels of heritability: whether raised together or apart, identical twins scored almost as alike as the same person tested twice.

Occupational interests show much lower rates of heritability—about 0.36—and shared environmental effects are significant—about 0.11—especially when compared with the zero effect on personality. The shared environment also plays a significant role in male juvenile delinquency and academic achievement. Taken together, personality, ability, interests, and attitudes make up what geneticists term the behavioral domain.

It could be that some shared environmental effects are invisible to behavioral geneticists because of the people they choose to test. Few twins studied are the products of extreme poverty or highly abusive backgrounds, nor are families with such a history usually allowed to adopt children; therefore, the findings really only apply to the broad middle class. Still, it's confounding to imagine that most families are such neutral environments; any gardener knows that rather small variations of water and fertilizer and soil acidity affect the development of far less complex organisms—are humans so indifferent to the environment they are planted in?

Social policy is largely a reflection of what we believe about how intelligence and personality are formed, and why people behave the way they do. It is not surprising, then, that concurrent with the resurgence of behavioral genetics in Western society over the past three decades, there has been a broad shift in political philosophy—one that assigns increased responsibility for individual behavior to the individual himself, not to his family, his schooling, his socioeconomic level. This is evident, for example, in the rise of unforgiving criminal sentencing standards and the cutback of innumerable social programs designed to lift people out of deprived circumstances. And yet, both liberals and conservatives remain obsessed with the influence of the environment on society and individual behavior; liberals continue to fight a rearguard action against racial and gender discrimination, the loss of access to education, the retreat of government from providing for social welfare, and so on; and conservatives still promote "family values" and seek to restrict government control of the economy while expanding legal restraints on certain behaviors, such as abortion and the use of illicit drugs. In the same manner, psychotherapists continue to assume that traumatic childhood experiences create repetitive patterns in people's lives, which can be arrested and changed. Educators continue to impose similar educational standards on children of varying talents. Social workers still work to train mothers how to interact with their children and job-seekers how to gain the skills they need. Employers strive to modify the workplace to accommodate demands for family leave, day care, and educational opportunities for their employees.

In other words, we continue to struggle to control our environments, despite the view of human behavior advanced by behavioral genetics, which suggests that the environment plays a diminished role in creating our personality and intelligence and in determining our behavior. Perhaps we struggle because the alternative is a kind of social and political nihilism that says that there is really very little we can do to change individual lives. Carried to an extreme, this view of human development suggests that the best, and perhaps only, way of improving society is by manipulating the gene pool.

The problem with the portrait of human nature that the behavioral geneticists have drawn for us is that it is at odds with our intuitive understanding of what makes us who we are. Clearly, it makes a difference in a person's identity if he is raised rich or poor, if he is a single child or one of many siblings, if he comes from a rural culture or an urban one, if his parents were happily married or divorced. Perhaps these differences aren't measurable on the Neuroticism scale, but if you propose that they don't shape human development, most people react with disbelief. Many studies have shown the connection between high IQ and having been raised in an intellectually stimulating home, for instance, or an abusive childhood and later violent behavior. How can these studies—as well as our intuitive understanding of the environmental influence on human development—accord with the persuasive studies showing that twins reared apart turn out to be about as much alike on most personality measurements as twins reared together, or that genetically unrelated siblings who are raised in the same family will turn out to be more like their biological parents than their adopted ones?

It is well known that children of divorce are somewhat more likely to become divorced themselves. They do less well in school and tend to have more discipline problems. The cause and the effect appear to be obvious and entirely environmental: children who have watched their parents' relationship fail haven't learned the skills to create a good marriage of their own. The social stigma associated with divorce, along with the financial hardships that typically follow the disintegration of the family and the stress of single parenting, would seem to explain the behavior problems of the children.

And yet, divorce also looks like a genetic disease. It runs in families. If an identical twin gets divorced, the chances that his co-twin will become divorced is about forty-five percent; for fraternal twins, the chances drop to thirty percent. That difference strongly suggests a genetic component to the risk of divorce. And in fact a large-scale 1992 study of Minnesota twins produced what now seems like predictable results: about fifty percent of the liability for divorce can be attributed to genetic factors, and zero for shared environmental effects. This is despite the fact that the parents' divorce is a striking feature of the shared environment. "Children whose parents divorce differ genetically from children whose parents do not divorce," the authors, Matt McGue and David Lykken, concluded. They propose that the genetic risk of divorce is a feature of many inherited personality traits, such as impulsiveness and neurotic behavior. Genes that create havoc in the parents' lives are likely to do the same in the lives of their children.

Divorce rates vary among cultures and over time. Of course, geneticists try to compare individual differences within particular populations—that's why the rate of divorce among Minnesota twins is compared with the average Minnesota rate, which is significantly lower than the national rate. But when geneticists focus on these individual differences within populations, they miss the fact that the cultural environment itself changes over the generations, often quickly and drastically, and divorce is an interesting example. Obviously divorce is going to be more frequent in a society where the laws permit it; it is also likely to occur more often in a highly sexualized culture where little social stigma attaches to failed marriages and where more couples are choosing not to have children. These extraordinary environmental changes that have taken place over the last several generations obviously affect the rate at which couples choose to separate. Granted that some individuals may be genetically more prone to divorce, this changed environment must act as a powerful reinforcement. But it is we who are remaking the divorce environment—through our laws and our behavior. Perhaps this compulsive manipulation of our cultural environment is a larger expression of the phenomenon that Sandra Scarr writes about on the individual level: we make our environment, and our collective genes drive our national experience. Both individually and culturally, the critical environment is the one that we create for ourselves.

To what extent, then, can we really say that genetic or environmental factors create divorce? We all know that it is easier and more acceptable to be divorced these days in most Western countries, and therefore divorce rates will be higher than in the past or in other cultures. Powerful environmental factors, such as religion, can also hold in check presumed genetic vulnerabilities. Perhaps we make changes in our culture in order to give expression to our genetic longing, whether it be for good or ill. The point is that even at this larger level, genes and the environment interact in a way that makes it difficult, and rather arbitrary, to parcel out percentages based on heritability correlations. Moreover, the entire process of evolution is one of genes adapting to the environment. In the larger sense, we do not make the environment; it makes us.

On the individual level, genes and the environment are similarly fused. The fact that experience itself appears to be partly heritable must be an expression of this complex entanglement. An example of this is that identical twins rate their parents more similarly for warmth than fraternal twins. This might be explained if we assume that identical twins are treated alike. Also, one supposes that parents who rate high in Extraversion and low in Neuroticism will provide warm and loving homes, so that the environment is only a natural expression of the parents' genetic disposition. What confounds this explanation is that identical twins raised apart also rate their experience of parental warmth very similarly, even though they have been raised by different people. Apparently, each twin evokes an experience—in this case, parental warmth—just by being who he is. But the experience of being raised by warm and loving parents is a significant environmental influence. So how can it be portioned out on one side of the ledger or the other? A starker example is a small study of adopted children whose biological parents are psychiatric patients. There was a significant association between the psychiatric status of the biological parent and the erratic rearing behavior of the adoptive parents. Presumably the inherited antisociality of the children elicits harsh and capricious parenting on the part of the adoptive parents. This supposedly environmental factor may in turn aggravate the antisocial behavior of the children. A number of factors that are usually described as environmental, such as the level of intellectual stimulation in the home, exposure to stress and trauma, and parental marital discord, also appear to be partly heritable. That is to say, children may elicit these environments whether they are raised in their biological home or an adopted one. But these are all the kinds of circumstances that environmentalists traditionally have pointed to as being powerfully formative in the creation of personality.

Even as different environments may produce (in the case of identical twins raised apart) similar personalities, the same environment may cause different reactions in different individuals. A study of more than four thousand pairs of twins who were veterans of Vietnam showed that those who were subjected to higher levels of combat were more likely to show signs of post-traumatic stress disorder—in other words, the environment creates the disorder. However, even among individuals who experienced similar levels of combat, the levels of PTSD varied widely. Identical twins were more alike in their reaction to combat stress than fraternal twins, demonstrating that the chances of suffering PTSD in combat are about thirty percent heritable. The point is that even in extreme environments, individuals have different levels of genetic vulnerability.

Perhaps the reader will forgive the obvious analogy that genes and the environment are like conjoined twins, distinct but inseparable. When we look at conjoined twins, are we seeing one organism or two? They share their circulation, their digestion, their general predicament of mutual dependency. They may have separate thoughts and desires and goals, but each has to negotiate with the other to achieve what he wants. In the same way, neither genes nor the environment can be neatly teased apart from the other and treated as an individual entity. Each is a part of a complicated amalgamation.

Twins have been used to tell us so much about our development, but the most troubling question they pose concerns our existential situation: that is to say, do we have free will? Is the concept of human freedom compromised by the existence of human doppelgängers—the separated twins who discover themselves in the middle of life and find that they have lived uncanny parallel existences?

Of course, as we have seen, identical twins can be quite different from each other; just to use the example of divorce again, an identical twin is still more likely not to get divorced if his twin is divorced—it's just that his chances are greater than for a fraternal twin and much greater than for the population as a whole. Even assuming that the identical twins have similar genetic propensities for stability and companionability, those propensities are handled differently most of the time. Alcoholism appears to be partly heritable, but even so, about half of the twins who are alcoholics have a twin who is not. Genetic traits for behavior are best understood as inclinations, not as mandates. There is still a measure of choice left to us about how we behave. We can change our behavior and the course of our lives, even though it may entail a struggle against our natural tendencies to be shy, or dominating, or overweight, or to smoke or drink too much. We all know the difficulty of reforming such traits. Realizing that we are born with these inclinations might even help us tame them, since we could see them as our responsibility, rather than as some wound that has been inflicted on us by our environment.

"A philosopher who was talking about twins said that maybe it's freedom that makes identical twins different," says Lindon J. Eaves, who is a human geneticist at the Medical College of Virginia. "Frankly, I don't believe that for a minute. It could be freedom that makes them alike." Eaves runs one of the largest twin studies in the world, the Virginia 30,000, which surveys 15,000 twin pairs and their relatives. He's also an Anglican priest and has reflected on the implications of behavior genetics for the doctrine of free will. "It's a mistake to define what is human simply by what psychologists can measure. We should define what is human by what humans do, and humans behave in ways that compel us to use the word 'freedom.' You get a sense of the limitations of psychology when you look at the instances we think of as quintessentially and most beautifully human, the astounding actions that seem to take human life into a new dimension—their creativity, or their way of dealing with oppression—I think that's where the concept of freedom lies. That's why I believe that the way we think about free will is really naive. Quite clearly it's crass to equate genetics with determinism and environmentalism with freedom. I think human freedom means something about the capacity of the human organism not to be pushed around or dominated by external circumstances. I would argue that evolution has given us our freedom. Freedom is the ability to stand up and transcend the limitations of the environment. That capacity is something that natural selection has placed in us, because it's adaptive. So I think it's probably genetic—the quest for freedom is genetic. I can't prove it, but I think it's probably a way forward."

Certainly one can view the environment as being just as constraining of free will as the genes. In the purely environmental perspective, there is no innate genetic drive demanding to be expressed. People are blank slates who are conditioned by environment to react in expectable ways. It's almost as if there is no self except for the shadow that is cast on the environment—and if there is no self that is aware of itself outside of the environment, how can we speak of freedom? "One way of looking at it is, if you're going to be pushed around, would you rather be pushed around by your environment, which is not you, or by your genes, which in some sense is who you are," says Eaves. Put so neatly, it makes one glad to exchange one oppressor for another.

But at the same time, it raises the question of what we mean by freedom. A trait that is genetically rooted seems to be more immutable than one that is conditioned by the environment—after all, we can change our environment, but a genetic predisposition seems to leave aside the possibility of free choice, or even consciousness of choice at all. Eaves seems to accept this idea when he speaks about subnormal personalities—people who are mentally retarded, for instance. "It's clear that for some people the options are fewer. The law recognizes that there are some people who for genetic or social reasons do not have what the normal human being is given—that is, freedom. We recognize that such people should be treated differently. This is the forensic recognition of diminished responsibility, which on the whole applies to extreme cases. But in what sense does it not apply to the rest of us? If you think in genetic terms, you have to say that diminished responsibility is a mutation on the gene that causes freedom."

Free will is what we call our conscious struggle to shape our own destinies. It refers to the struggle with our selves, with the kind of people that we chose to become. Implicit in the concept of free will is the wishful notion that we can leap over the limitations of our environment and our genes, which of course we cannot do, any more than a child can jump off the bed and start to fly. Genetically, we can only make the best of what we have. People who are aware of their natures are constantly wrestling with tendencies they recognize as ingrained or inborn. That doesn't mean that they have no choice in directing those tendencies toward better or worse uses.

Finally, twins raise the question of what the self really is. Being genetically identical with another human being encroaches on our sense of being unique in the world, of having thoughts and desires and experiences that no one else knows about or can possibly share. But if tomorrow you suddenly turn a corner and find yourself looking into a human mirror—your identical separated sibling—the chances are that you will have an astonishing amount in common, despite the fact that you have lived in different homes and led entirely separate lives. It is the most narcissistic encounter imaginable—to be able to stand aside and really look at your almost-self, to talk to someone else who is inside the same physical package, to experience your almost-self as others must experience you. No doubt it is exhilarating to discover another individual who is uniquely able to understand you, who seems to anticipate your thoughts before you form them. The saga of how each of you contested with life to arrive at similar places with similar points of view is an affirmation of who you were intended to be. Perhaps there is an element of the uncanny in your new relationship; you may have always thought there was something uncompleted in your life that now is resoundingly answered and fulfilled. The power of this widespread fantasy is a testament to how much we long to be understood on a deeper level than ordinary love and friendship can provide.

But at the same time, seeing yourself replicated is a shocking confrontation with the finite nature of who you really are. It is so much easier to see those limitations in others, but in your identical twin you can see the reflected limitations in yourself. You see how nature has shaped you; you grasp at once that your abilities and talents, however broad, are circumscribed. The nature of this shock is similar to those of the first time you hear yourself on a recording or see yourself on television. Of course, it's not you but a human approximation. You notice at once the differences between you, the subtle non-you things that are just a bit off, although a bystander may not be able to tell the two of you apart. After you've explored the variety of ways that you are alike, it is the differences between you that capture your attention. Perhaps that is a way of holding on to your separateness, your particular identity.

Now that you are no longer a singleton but something rare and special, an identical twin, you will be courted by researchers who want to measure every detail of your physical and psychological beings. You will discover that much of what you thought was unique to you has actually been franchised to another individual. Your bodies resemble each other and so do your minds. Let us say you are as alike as two different McDonald's restaurants in separate cities—the same architecture, the same inner decor, the same employee uniforms, the same menu. The environment outside may be Des Moines or Dallas, but the structure of the restaurant is the same. The experience of being in either place is hauntingly unvaried.

Even if tests can't tell you apart, you know you're not the same person, despite the weird commonalities and the coincidences that make it seem as if you are inhabiting the same psychic space. But some of your selfhood has been appropriated. There is one side of you that wants your twin to be exactly like you in every detail, a perfect replica, but another side of you is struggling for air. You feel like you are being smothered by the sameness. Your specialness is being erased with every thrilling landmark of recognition.

After you finish the tests, you and your separated twin decide to indulge a fantasy that only identical twins can actually attempt: you will trade lives. You return not to your own home and job and family but to your twin's. It would be a rare set of twins who are so much alike as adults that loved ones could not tell them apart, but in your case, you and your twin are so similar that no one will guess what you're up to. When you walk into your twin's life, it seems stylistically the same. You've made similar choices in your career, and although love choices are notoriously varied even among identical twins, in this case you find your twin has made an acceptable match. You can now live out your life as someone else, while someone else occupies the place that once was yours.

Who are you now?

You are yourself. You might change everything about your identity, but you cannot change your awareness of yourself as a separate being. The fantasized twin that we carry about in our minds is not only an idealized partner in the experience of being who we are, he is also a means of escape from the life we are living. Twins have often told us that theirs is the most precious relationship imaginable, the closest experience one can have of being with another. Just by being twins, they have been able to reveal many answers to the riddles of existence. But they also show us that no matter how tantalizingly alike we may be, no one crosses the boundary between being alike and being the same. We might, as in this fantasy, be able to exchange lives, but we cannot exchange selves. There is finally no escape from being the people we were born to be.

Bibliography

Abrams, S., "Disposition and the environment," in Solnit, A.J., Neubauer, P.B., Abrams, S., Dowling, S.D. (eds), *The Psychoanalytic Study of the Child, 49th Edition,* New Haven, Yale University Press, 1994

Abrams, S. and Neubauer, P.B., "Hartmann's vision: identical twins and developmental organizations," in Solnit, A.J., Neubauer, P.B., Abrams, S., Dowling, S.D. (eds), *The Psychoanalytic Study of the Child, 49th Edition,* New Haven, Yale University Press, 1994

Ainslie, R., *The Psychology of Twinship,* Northvale, Jason Aronson, 1997

Aldhous, P., "The promise and pitfalls of molecular genetics," *Science,* 1992, 257:5067:164

———, "Burt files reopened," *Science,* 1992, 354:97

———, "Psychologists rethink Burt," *Science,* 1992, 356:5

Allgulander, C., Nowak, J., Rice, J.P., "Psychopathology and treatment of 30,344 twins in Sweden. II. Heritability estimates of psychiatric diagnosis and treatment in 12,884 pairs," *Acta Psychiatr. Scand.,* 1991, 83:12–15

Alper, J.S. "The allure of genetic explanations," *Br. Med. J.,* 1992, 305:666

Alvarado, D., "Prenatal testing: the search for healthy babies offers expectant parents multiple choices," *Dallas Morning News* 15 March 1993

Andreasen, N.C., Ehrhardt, J.C., Crossett, J.H.W., et al., "Letters to the Editor," *Arch. Gen. Psychiatry,* 1987, 44:673–6

Ansley, D., "Aging twins offer clues to late-onset illness," *Science,* 1993, 259:5103:1826

Arvey, R.D., Bouchard Jr., T.J., Segal, N.L., Abraham, L.M., "Job satisfaction: environmental and genetic components," *Journal of Applied Psychology,* 1989, 74:2:187–92

Ashenfelter, O. and Krueger, A., "Estimates of the economic return to schooling from a new sample of twins," *American Economic Review,* 1994, 84:5:1158–73

Bailey, J.M. and Pillard, R.C., "A genetic study of male sexual orientation," *Arch. Gen. Psychiatry,* 1991, 48:1089–96

Bailey, J.M., Pillard, R.C., Neale, M.C., Agyei, Y., 'Heritable factors influence sexual orientation in women," *Arch. Gen. Psychiatry,* 1993, 50:217–23

Bajoria, R., Wigglesworth, J., Fisk, N.M., "Angio-architecture of monochromatic placenta in relation to the twin-twin transfusion syndrome," *Israel J. Obstet. Gynaecol.,* 1994, 5:3 (Supplement)

Baker, L.A., Cesa, I.L., Gats, M., Mellins, C., "Genetic and environmental influences on positive and negative affect: support for a two-factor theory," *Psychology and Aging,* 1992, 7:1:158–63

Baker, L.A. and Clark, R., "Genetic origins of behavior: implications for counselors," *Journal of Counseling and Development,* 1990, 68:597–600

Baker, L.A. and Daniels, D., "Nonshared environmental influences and personality differences in adult twins," *Journal of Personality and Social Psychology,* 1990, 58:1:103–10

Baker, L.A., Reynolds, C., Phelps, E., "Biometrical analysis of individual growth curves," *Behavior Genetics,* 1992, 22:2:253–63

Balaban, E., "Behavior genetics: Galen's prophecy or Malpighi's legacy?" Written for the Banbury Center conference on Genetics and Human Behavior, 5–8 March 1995

Bartfai, A., Pedersen, N.L., Asarnow, R.F., Schalling, D., "Genetic factor for the span of apprehension test: a study of normal twins," *Psychiatry Research,* 1991, 38:115–24

Baumrind, D., "The average expectable environment is not good enough: a response to Scarr," *Child Development,* 1993, 64: 1299–317

Behrman, J.R., Rosenzweig, M.R., Taubman, P., "Endowments and the allocation of schooling in the family and in the marriage market: the twins experiment," *Journal of Political Economy,* 1994, 102:6:1131–74

Bereiter, C., "The future of individual differences," in Jensen, A.R. (ed.), *Environment, Heredity, and Intelligence,* Montpelier, Capital City Press, 1969

Berenbaum, H., Oltmanns, T.F., Gottesman, I.I., "Hedonic capacity in schizophrenics and their twins," *Psychological Medicine,* 1990, 20:2:367–74

Bergeman, C.S., Plomin, R., Pedersen, N.L., McClearn, G.E., Nesselroade, J.R., "Genetic and environmental influences on social support: the Swedish Adoption/Twin Study of Aging," *Journal of Gerontology,* 1990, 45:3:101–6

Betsworth, D.G., Bouchard Jr., T.J., Cooper, C.R., et al., "Genetic and environmental influences on vocational interests assessed using adoptive and biological families and twins reared apart and together," *Journal of Vocational Behavior,* 1994, 44:263–78

Biale, R., "Twins have unique developmental aspects," *Brown University Child Behavior and Development Letter,* 1989, 5:6:1

Blinkhorn, S., "Was Burt stitched up?" *Nature,* 1989, 340: 439–40

Boklage, C.E., "On the distribution of nonrighthandedness among twins and their families," *Acta Genet. Med. Gemellol.,* 1981, 30:167–87

———, "On the timing of monozygotic twinning events," in *Twin Research 3: Twin Biology and Multiple Pregnancy,* New York, Alan R. Liss, 1981

———, "Differences in protocols of cranofacial developmental related to twinship and zygosity, *Journal of Craniofacial Genetics and Developmental Biology*, 1984, 4:151–69

———, "Race, zygosity, and mortality among twins: interaction of myth and method," *Acta Genet. Med. Gemellol.*, 1987, 36:275–88

———, "The organization of the oocyte and embryogenesis in twinning and fusion malformations," *Acta Genet. Med. Gemellol.*, 1987, 36:421–31

———, "Twinning, nonrighthandedness, and fusion malformations: evidence for heritable causal elements held in common," *American Journal of Medical Genetics*, 1987, 28: 67–84

———, "Survival probability of human conceptions from fertilization to term," *Int. J. Fertil.*, 1990, 35:2:75–94

———, "Method and meaning in the analysis of developmental asymmetries," *J. Hum. Ecol. Special Issue*, 1992, 2:147–56

———, "The frequency and survival probability of natural twin conceptions," in Keith, L.G., et al. (eds), *Multiple Pregnancy: Epidemiology, Gestation, and Perinatal Outcome*, London, Parthenon Publishing, 1995

———, "Effects of a behavioral rhythm on conception probability and pregnancy outcome," *Human Reproduction*, 1996, 11:10:2276–84

Boklage, C.E., Kirby, C.F., Zincone, L.H., "Annual and subannual rhythms in human conception rates: I. Effective correction and use of public record LMP dates," *Int. J. Fertil.*, 1992, 37:2:74–81

Boklage, C.E., Zincone, L.H., Kirby Jr., C.F., "Annual and subannual rhythms in human conception rates: time-series analyses show annual and weekday but no monthly rhythms in daily counts for last normal menses," *Human Reproduction*, 1992, 7:7:899–905

Boomsma, D.I. and Somsen, R.J.M., "Reaction time measured in a choice reaction time and a double task condition: a small twin study," *Person. Individ. Diff.*, 1991, 12:6:519–22

Boor, M., "Genetic correlations are not squared to determine common variance," *American Psychologist,* 1973, 28:1139

Bouchard Jr., T.J., "Do environmental similarities explain the similarity in intelligence of identical twins reared apart?," *Intelligence,* 1983, 7:175–84

———, "Twins reared together and apart: what they tell us about human diversity," in Fox, S. (ed), *Individuality and Determinism: Chemical and Biological Bases,* New York, Plenum, 1984

———, "The genetic architecture of human intelligence," in Vernon, P.A. (ed), *Biological Approaches to the Study of Human Intelligence,* Norwood, Ablex, 1993

———, "Genes, environment, and personality," *Science,* 1994, 264:1700–1

———, "Ideological obstacles to genetic research: tales from the nature-nurture wars," paper presented to the seminar "Science and the Powers," 16 March 1994, Stockholm, Sweden

———, "IQ similarity in twins reared apart: finding and responses to critics," in Sternberg, R. and Grigorenko, E. (eds), *Intelligence, Heredity, and Environment,* New York, Cambridge University Press, 1994

———, "Breaking the last taboo," *Contemporary Psychology,* 1995, 40:5

———, "The genetics of personality," in Blum, K. and Noble, E.P. (eds), *Handbook of Psychoneurogenetics,* Boca Raton, CRC Press, 1995

———, "Meta-analysis and Model Fitting—Comment on Devlin et al.," *Nature,* in press

Bouchard Jr., T.J., Lykken, D.T., McGue, M., Segal, N.L., Tellegen, A., "Sources of human psychological differences: the Minnesota study of twins reared apart," *Science,* 1990, 250: 223–8

Bouchard Jr., T.J. and McGue, M., "Genetic and rearing environmental influences on adult personality: an analysis of adopted twins reared apart," *Journal of Personality,* 1990, 58:1:263–92

Bouchard Jr., T.J. and Propping, P. (eds), "Report of the Dahlem Workshop on 'What are the mechanisms mediating the genetic and environmental determinants of behavior?' " in *Twins as a Tool of Behavioral Genetics,* Chichester, John Wiley, 1993

Bower, B., "Same family, different lives," *Science News,* 1991, 140:23:376

Boxer, S., "Where twins diverge: on human tragedies," *New York Times,* 25 June 1996

Bracha, H.S., "On concordance for tuberculosis and schizophrenia," *Am. J. Psychiatry,* 1986, 143:12:1634

Brazziel, W.F., "A letter from the south," in Jensen, A.R. (ed), *Environment, Heredity, and Intelligence,* Montpelier, Capital City Press, 1969

Brooks, A., Fulker, D.W., DeFries, J.C., "Reading performance and general cognitive ability: a multivariate genetic analysis of twin data," *Person. Individ. Diff.,* 1990, 11:2:141–6

Bryan, E., "The intrauterine hazards of twins," *Archives of Disease in Childhood,* 1986, 61:1044–5

———, *Twins and Higher Multiple Births: A Guide to Their Nature and Nurture,* London, Edward Arnold, 1992

———, "Prenatal and perinatal influences on twin children: implications for behavioral studies," in Bouchard, T.J. and Propping, P. (eds) *Twins as a Tool of Behavioral Genetics* Chichester, John Wiley, 1993

———, "Trends in twinning rates; conference on genetic epidemiology of twins and twinning," *Lancet,* 1994, 343:1151–2

———, "Genetic epidemiology of twins and twinning," *Multiple Births Foundation Newsletter,* 1994, 24:1

Bryan, E., Little, J., Burn, J., "Congenital anomalies in twins," *Baillière's Clinical Obstetrics and Gynaecology,* 1987, 1:3: 697–721

Burn, J., "Twins and twinning," in Chervenak, F.A., Isaacson, G.C., Campbell, S. (eds) *Ultrasound in Obstetrics and Gynecology,* Boston, Little Brown, 1993

Burn, J., Povey, S., Boyd, Y., et al., "Duchenne muscular dystrophy in one of monozygotic twin girls," *Journal of Medical Genetics,* 1986, 23:494–500

Burt C., *The Young Delinquent,* University of London Press, 1925

———, *The Subnormal Mind,* Oxford, Oxford University Press, 1935

———, *The Backward Child,* University of London Press, 1937

———, "The genetic determination of differences in intelligence: a study of monozygotic twins reared together and apart," *British Journal of Psychology,* 1966, 57:137–53

———, "Inheritance of general intelligence," *American Psychologist,* 1972, 27:3:175–90

Carey, G., "Genes, fears, phobias, and phobic disorders," *Journal of Counseling and Development,* 1990, 68:628–32

Carmelli, D., Swan, G.E., Robinette, D., Fabsitz, R., "Genetic influence on smoking—a study of male twins," *New England Journal of Medicine,* 1992, 327:829–33

Carmelli, D., Cardon, L.R., Fabsitz, R., "Clustering of hypertension, diabetes, and obesity in adult male twins: same genes or same environments?" *Am. J. Hum. Genet.,* 1994, 55:566–73

Carmelli, D., Robinette, D., Fabsitz, R., "Concordance, discordance, and prevalence of hypertension in World War II male veteran twins," *Journal of Hypertension,* 1994, 12:323–8

Carmelli, D., Swan, G.E., Page, W.F., Christian, J.C., "World War II–veteran male twins who are discordant for alcohol consumption: 24-year mortality," *American Journal of Public Health,* 1995, 85:1:99–101

Carter-Saltzman, L., Scarr, S., Barker, W., "Do these co-twins really live together? An assessment of the validity of the home index as a measure of family socio-economic status," *Educational and Psychological Measurement,* 1975, 35:427–35

Cassill, K., *Twins: Nature's Amazing Mystery,* New York, Atheneum, 1982

———, "The phantom twin: there's eerie evidence that many of us shared the womb with brother or sister who vanished before birth," *Health*, 1983, 15:50

Central Intelligence Agency, "Extrasensory electroencephalographic induction between identical twins," unsigned, undated CIA document

Chapman, A., "First person: a tale of two sisters," *Guardian*, 12 March 1993

Chipuer, H.M., Rovine, M.J., Plomin, R., "LISREL modeling: genetic and environmental influences on IQ revisited," *Intelligence*, 1990, 14:1:11029

Chitkara, B., MacDonald, A., Reveley, A.M., "Twin birth and adult psychiatric disorder: an examination of the case records of the Maudsley Hospital," *British Journal of Psychiatry*, 1988, 152:391–8

Cimons, M., "Multiple-baby births quadruple since 1980," *Austin American-Statesman*, 2 February 1997

Claridge, G. and Hewitt, J.K., "A biometrical study of schizotypy in a normal population," *Person. Individ. Diff.*, 1987, 8:3: 303–12

Clark, C., Klonoff, H., Tyhurst, J.S., Li, D., Martin, W., Pate, B.D., "Regional cerebral glucose metabolism in three sets of identical twins with psychotic symptoms," *Canadian Journal of Psychiatry*, 1989, 34:4:263–70

Corney, G., "The biology of twinning," *Journal of Obstetrics and Gynecology*, 1987, 8:70–86

Crawford, C., Smith, M., Krebs, D., "Sociobiology: environmentalist and discursive," *Contemporary Psychology*, 1990, 35: 4:410

———, "Sociobiology: is it still too emotional to handle?," *Contemporary Psychology*, 1990, 35:4: 408–10

Creinin, M. and Keith, L.G., "The Yoruba contribution to our understanding of the twinning process," *Journal of Reproductive Medicine*, 1987, 34:6:379–87

Cronbach, L.J., "Heredity, environment, and educational policy," in Jensen, A.R. (ed), *Environment, Heredity, and Intelligence,* Montpelier, Capital City Press, 1969

Crow, J.F., "Genetic theories and influences: comments on the value of diversity," in Jensen, A.R. (ed), *Environment, Heredity, and Intelligence,* Montpelier, Capital City Press, 1969

Cummings, M., *Human Heredity, 3rd Edition,* St. Paul, West Publishing, 1993

Danis, R.P. and Keith, L.G., "Some observations concerning leukemia in twins," *Acta Genet. Med. Gemellol.,* 1982, 31: 173–7

Depp, R., Keith, L.G., Sciarra, J.J., "The Northwestern University Twin Study VII: the mode of delivery in twin pregnancy North American considerations," *Acta Genet. Med. Gemellol.,* 1988, 37:11–18

Derom, C., Vlietinck, R., Derom, R., Van Den Berghe, H., Thiery, M., "Increased monozygotic twinning rate after ovulation induction," *Lancet,* 30 May 1987

Devlin, B., Daniels, M., Roeder, K., "The heritability of IQ," *Nature,* 31 July 1997, 388, 468–71

Devlin, B., Fienberg, S., Resnick, D., Roeder, K. (eds) *Intelligence, Genes, and Success,* New York, Copernicus, 1997

Diamond, M., "Brief communication: sexual identity, monozygotic twins reared in discordant sex roles and a BBC follow-up," *Archives of Sexual Behavior,* 1982, 11:2:181–7

Diamond, M. and Sigmundson, H.K., "Sex reassignment at birth: long-term review and clinical implications," *Arch. Pediatr. Adolesc. Med.,* 1997, 151:298–304

DiLalla, L.F., Thompson, L.A., Plomin, R., Philips, K., Fagan III, J.F., Hagan, M.M., Cyphers, L.H., Fulker, D.W., "Infant predictors of preschool and adult IQ: a study of infant twins and their parents," *Developmental Psychology,* 1990, 26:5:759–69

Dorfman, D.D., "The Cyril Burt question: new findings," *Science,* 1978, 201:1177–86

Dworkin, R.H., "Patterns of sex differences in negative symptoms and social functioning consistent with separate dimensions of schizophrenic psychopathology," *Am. J. Psychiatry,* 1990, 347–9

———, Lenzenweger, M.F., Moldin, S.O., Skillings, G.F., Levick, S.E., "A multidimensional approach to the genetics of schizophrenia," *Am. J. Psychiatry,* 1988, 145:9: 1077–83

Eaves, L.J., Eysenck, H.J., Martin, N.G., *Genes, Culture, and Personality: An Empirical Approach,* London, Academic Press, 1989

Eckert, E.D., Bouchard Jr., T.J., Bohlen, J., Heston, L.L., "Homosexuality in monozygotic twins reared apart," *British Journal of Psychiatry,* 1986, 148:421–5

Elkind, D., "Piagetian and Psychometric Conceptions of Intelligence," in Jensen, A.R. (ed), *Environment, Heredity, and Intelligence,* Montpelier, Capital City Press, 1969

Ellis, L. and Hoffman, H., *Crime in Biological, Social, and Moral Contexts,* New York, Praeger, 1990

Ellis, M.V. and Robbins, E.S., "In celebration of nature: a dialogue with Jerome Kagan," *Journal of Counseling and Development,* 1990, 68:623–7

Ellis, R.F., Berger, G.S., Keith, L., Depp, R., "The Northwestern University Multihospital Twin Study: II. Mortality of first versus second twins," *Acta Genet. Med. Gemellol.,* 1979, 28:347–52

Farber, S.L., *Identical Twins Reared Apart,* New York, Basic Books, 1981

Farmer, A.E., McGuffin, P., Gottesman, I.I., "Twin concordance for DSM-II schizophrenia: scrutinizing the validity of the definition," *Arch. Gen. Psychiatry,* 1987, 44:634–41

Fisk, N.M. and Bryan, E.M., "Routine prenatal determination of chorionicity in multiple gestation: a plea to the obstetrician," *British Journal of Obstetrics and Gynaecology,* 1993, 100: 975–7

Fletcher, R., *Science, Ideology, and the Media: the Cyril Burt Scandal,* New Brunswick, NJ, Transaction Publishers, 1991

Galton, F., "The history of twins as a criterion of the relative powers of nature and nurture," *Fraser's Magazine*, 1875, 92, 566–576

———, *Hereditary Genius: An Inquiry into its Laws and Consequences*, London, Macmillan, 1883

———, *Inquiries into Human Faculty and Its Development*, New York, Macmillan, 1883

Gatz, M., "Interpreting behavioral genetic results: suggestions for counselors and clients," *Journal of Counseling and Development*, 1990, 68:601–5

Gedda, L., *Twins in History and Science*, Springfield, Charles C. Thomas, 1961

Gleeson, C., Hay, D.A., Johnston, C.J., Theobald, T.M., " 'Twins in school': an Australia-wide program," *Acta Genet. Med. Gemellol.*, 1990, 39:231–44

Giannakoulopoulos, X., Sepulveda, W., Kourtis, P., Glover, V., Fisk, N.M., "Fetal plasma cortisol and β-endorphin response to intrauterine needling," *Lancet*, 1994, 344:77–81

Gillie, O., "Crucial data was faked by eminent psychologist," *Sunday Times*, (London), 24 October 1976

Golbin, A., Golbin, Y., Keith, L., Keith, D., "Mirror imaging in twins: biological polarization—an evolving hypothesis," *Acta Genet. Med. Gemellol.*, 1993, 42:237–43

Goldberg, T.E., Ragland, D., Torrey, E.F., Gold, J.M., Bigelow, L.B., Weinberger, D.R., "Neuropsychological assessment of monozygotic twins discordant for schizophrenia," *Arch. Gen. Psychiatry*, 1990, 47:1066–72

Goldman, G.A., Feldberg, D.D., Ashkensazi, J., et al. "The vanishing fetus: a report of 17 cases of triplets and quadruplets," *J. Perinat. Med.*, 1989, 17:157–62

Goldsmith, H.H. and Campos, J.J., "The structure of temperamental fear and pleasure in infants: a psychometric perspective," *Child Development*, 1990, 61:1944–64

Goodhart, C.B., "Burt files reopened," *Nature*, 1992, 355:103

Goodman, R. and Stevenson, J., "A twin study of hyperactivity–I. An examination of hyperactivity scores and categories derived from Rutter teacher and parent questionnaires," *J. Child Psychol. Psychiatr.*, 1989, 30:5:671–89

———, "A twin study of hyperactivity–II. The etiological role of genes, family relationships, and perinatal adversity," *J. Child Psychol. Psychiatr.*, 1989, 30:5: 691–709

Goodship, J., Carter, J., Burn, J., "X-Inactivation patterns in monozygotic and dizygotic female twins," *American Journal of Medical Genetics*, in press

Gottesman, I.I., "Differential inheritance of the psychoneuroses," *Eugenics Quarterly*, 1962, 9:223–7

Gottesman, I.I. and Bertelsen, A., "Confirming unexpressed genotypes for schizophrenia," *Arch. Gen. Psychiatry*, 1989, 46:867–72

Gould, S.J., *The Mismeasure of Man*, New York, W.W. Norton, 1981

Griffiths, A., Miller, J., Suzuki, D., Lewontin, R., Gelbart, W., *An Introduction to Genetic Analysis, 5th Edition*, New York, W.H. Freeman, 1993

Hall, J.G. and Lopez-Rangel, E., "Newly recognized mechanisms of discordance and their role in twins and twinning," unpublished manuscript

———, "Review of twins and twinning and a hypothesis concerning monozygotic twins," unpublished manuscript

Hartmann, H., *Essays on Ego Psychology*, New York, International Universities Press, 1964

Hawkes, N., "Tracing Burt's descent to scientific fraud," *Science*, 1979, 205:673–5

Hearnshaw, L., *Cyril Burt, Psychologist*, London, Hodder and Stoughton, 1979

Herrnstein, R., "IQ," *Atlantic Monthly*, September 1971, 43–64

———, *IQ and the Meritocracy*, Boston, Atlantic Monthly Press, 1973

Herrnstein, R. and Murray, C., *The Bell Curve*, New York, Free Press, 1994

Hirschfeld, L.A., "The heritability of identity: children's understanding of the cultural biology of race," *Child Development,* in press

Holden, C., "Twins reunited," *Science,* 1980, 55–9

Holzman, P.S., Kringen, E., Matthysse, S., et al., "A single dominant gene can account for eye tracking dysfunctions and schizophrenia in offspring of discordant twins," *Arch. Gen. Psychiatry,* 1988, 45:641–7

Horgan, J., "Eugenics revisited," *Scientific American,* 1993, 268:6:122–31

Hoyme, H.E., Higginbottom, M.C., Jones, K.L., "Vascular etiology of disruptive structural defects in monozygotic twins," *Pediatrics,* 1981, 67:2:288–91

Hunt, J. McV., "Has compensatory education failed? Has it been attempted?" in Jensen, A.R. (ed), *Environment, Heredity, and Intelligence,* Montpelier, Capital City Press, 1969

Huter, O., Bezinka, C., Busch, G., Pfaller, C., "The 'vanishing twin,' " *Geburtshilfe Frauenkeilkd.,* 1990, 50:12:989–92

Jackson, J., "Human behavioral genetics, Scarr's theory, and her views on interventions: a critical review and commentary on their implications for African American children," *Child Development,* 1993, 64:1318–32

Jensen, A.R., "How much can we boost IQ and scholastic achievement?," in Jensen, A.R. (ed), *Environment, Heredity, and Intelligence,* Montpelier, Capital City Press, 1969

———, "Reducing the heredity-environment uncertainty," in Jensen, A.R. (ed), *Environment, Heredity, and Intelligence,* Montpelier, Capital City Press, 1969

———, "Scientific fraud or false accusations? The case of Cyril Burt," in Miller, D.J. and Hersen, M. (eds), *Research Fraud in the Behavioral and Biomedical Sciences,* New York, John Wiley, 1992

Jimison, S., "Fetus removed from a 3-month-old girl is 'perfectly formed,' " *Weekly World News,* 24 March 1987

Joynson, R.B., *The Burt Affair,* London, Routledge, 1989

Juel-Nielsen, N., *Individual and Environment: Monozygotic Twins Reared Apart,* New York, International Universities Press, 1981

Kagan, J.S., "Inadequate evidence and illogical conclusions," in Jensen, A.R. (ed), *Environment, Heredity, and Intelligence,* Montpelier, Capital City Press, 1969

Kamin, L., *The Science and Politics of IQ,* New York, Halsted Press, 1974

———, "Behind the curve," *Scientific American,* February 1995, 99–103

Kaminer, Y., Feingold, M., Lyons, K., "Single case study: bulimia in a pair of monozygotic twins," *Journal of Nervous and Mental Disease,* 1988, 176:4:246–8

Karlsson, J.L., "Partly dominant transmission of schizophrenia in Iceland," *British Journal of Psychiatry,* 1988, 152:324–9

Keith, L., and Brown, E., "Cancer in twins: concordance or discordance?" *Acta Genet. Med. Gemellol.,* 1970, 19:61–4

———, "Malignant tumors among twins: a study of divergent views," *Acta Genet. Med. Gemellol.,* 1970, 19:576–83

Keith, L., Brown, E.R., Ames, B., Stotsky, M., "Possible obstetric factors affecting leukemia in twins," *Bibliotheca Haematologica,* 1976, 43:221–3

Keith, L., Brown, E.R., Ames, B., Stotsky, M., Keith, D.M., "Leukemia in twins: antenatal and postnatal factors," *Acta Genet. Med. Gemellol.,* 1976, 25:336–41

Keith, L., Brown, E.R., Fields, C., Stepto, R., "Age group differences of twins with leukemia," *Bibliotheca Haematologica,* 1971, 39:1125–35

Keith, L., Ellis, R., Berger, S., Depp, R., "The Northwestern University Multihospital Twin Study I. A description of 588 twin pregnancies and associated pregnancy loss, 1971–1975," *American Journal of Obstetrics and Gynecology,* 1980, 138:7:781–9

Keith, L.G., Ameli, S., Keith, D.M., "The Northwestern University Twin Study I: Overview of the international literature," *Acta Genet. Med. Gemellol.*, 1988, 37:55–63

Keith, L.G., Depp, R., Method, M.W., et al., "The Northwestern University Twin Study V: Twin deliveries at Prentice Woman's Hospital and Maternity Center, 1978–83," *Acta Genet. Med. Gemellol.*, 1988, 37:1–10

Keith, L.G., Keith, D.M., Golbin, A., Golbin, I., "Mirror imaging in twins: biological polarization—an evolving hypothesis," *Acta Genet. Med. Gemellol.*, 1995, 42:237–43

Keith, L.G., Lopez-Zeno, J., Luke, B., "Twin gestation," in Droegemueller, W. and Sciarra, J.J. (eds), *Gynecology and Obstetrics, Revised Edition,* Philadelphia, J.B. Lippincott, 1991

———, "Triplet and higher order pregnancies," *Contemporary Obstetrics and Gynecology,* June 1993, 36–50

Keith, L.G. and Luke, B., "Comments on the 'epidemic' of multiple pregnancies," *Israel Journal of Obstetrics and Gynecology,* 1993, 4:2:79–84

Keith, L.G., Papiernik, E., Luke, B., "The costs of multiple pregnancy," *Int. J. Gynecol. Obstet.*, 1991, 36:109–14

Keith, L.G., Papiernik, E., Keith, D.M., Luke, B. (eds), *Multiple Pregnancy: Epidemiology, Gestation, and Perinatal Outcome,* London, Parthenon Publishing, 1995

Kelly, M.P., et al., "Human chorionic gonadotropin rise in normal and vanishing twin pregnancies," *Fertil. Steril.*, 1991, 56:2:221–4

Kendler, K.S., "Twin studies of psychiatric illness: current status and future directions," *Arch. Gen. Psychiatry,* 1993, 50: 905–15

Kendler, K.S., Heath, A.C., Martin, N.G., Eaves, L.J., "Symptoms of anxiety and symptoms of depression," *Arch. Surg.* 1987, 122:451–7

Kendler, K.S., Kessler, R.C., Neale, M.C., Heath, A.C., Phil, D., Eaves, L.J., "The prediction of major depression in women:

toward an integrated etiologic model," *Am. J. Psychiatry,* 1993, 150:8:1139–48

Kendler, K.S., Neale, M.C., Heath, A.C., Kessler, R.C., Eaves, L.J., "A twin-family study of alcoholism in women," *Am. J. Psychiatry,* 1994, 151:5:707–15

Kendler, K.S., Neale, M.C., Kessler, R.C., Heath, A.C., Eaves, L.J., "A population-based twin study of major depression in women," *Arch. Gen. Psychiatry,* 1992, 49:257–66

———, "Major depression and generalized anxiety disorder," *Arch. Gen. Psychiatry,* 1992, 49:716–22

———, "A longitudinal twin study of 1-year prevalence of major depression in women," *Arch. Gen. Psychiatry,* 1993, 50:843–52

Kendler, K.S., Silberg, J.L., Neale, M.C., Kessler, R.C., Heath, A.C., Eaves, L.J., "The family history method: whose psychiatric history is measured?" *Am. J. Psychiatry,* 1991, 148:11: 1501–4

Kendler, K.S., Tsuang, M.T., Hays, P., "Age at onset in schizophrenia," *Arch. Gen. Psychiatry,* 1987, 44:881–90

Kevles, D.J., "Annals of eugenics: a secular faith—I," *New Yorker,* 8 October 1984

———, "Annals of eugenics: a secular faith—II," *New Yorker,* 15 October 1984

———, "Annals of eugenics: a secular faith—III," *New Yorker,* 22 October 1984

———, "Annals of eugenics: a secular faith—IV," *New Yorker,* 29 October 1984

Knobloch, W.H., Leavenworth, N.M., Bouchard Jr., T.J., Echert, E.D., "Eye findings in twins reared apart," *Ophthalmic Pediatrics and Genetics,* 1985, 5:12:59–66

Koch, H.L., *Twins and Twin Relations,* Chicago, University of Chicago Press, 1966

Kringlen, E. and Cramer, G., "Offspring of monozygotic twins discordant for schizophrenia," *Arch. Gen. Psychiatry,* 1989, 46:873–7

Kurosawa, K., Kuromaru, R., Imaizumi, K., et al. "Monozygotic twins with discordant sex," *Acta Genet. Med. Gemellol.*, 1992, 41:4:301–10

LaBuda, M., DeFries, J.C., Fulker, D.W., "Genetic and environment covariance structures among WISC-R subtests: a twin study," *Intelligence*, 1987, 11:233–44

Lagnado, L.M. and Dekal, S.C., *Children of the Flames: Dr Joseph Mengele and the Untold Story of the Twins of Auschwitz*, London, Sidgwick and Jackson, 1991

Landy, H.J. and Hill, M.C., "Ultrasound of twin gestations," *Ultrasound Quarterly*, 1989, 7:2:107–32

Landy, H.J., Keith, L., Keith, D., "The vanishing twin," *Acta Genet. Med. Gemellol.*, 1982, 31:179–94

Landy, H.J. and Nies, B.M., "The vanishing twin," in Keith, L.G. and Papiernik, E. (eds), *Multiple Pregnancy: Epidemiology. Gestation and Perinatal Outcome*, London, Parthenon Publishing, 1995

Landy, H.J., Weiner, S., Corson, S.L., et al., "The 'vanishing twin:' ultrasonic assessment of fetal disappearance in the first trimester," *Am. J. Obstet. Gynecol.*, 1986, 155:14–19

Landy, H. and Weingold, A.B., "Management of a multiple gestation complicated by an antepartum fetal demise," *Obstet. Gynecol. Survey*, 1989, 44:171–6

Lane, C., "The tainted sources of 'The Bell Curve,' " *New York Review of Books*, 1 December 1994

Lang, J.S., "Happiness is a reunited set of twins," *U.S. News and World Report*, 13 April 1987

Lange, J., *Crime as Destiny*, London, G. Allen and Unwin, 1931

Leder, J.M., "Adult sibling rivalry," *Psychology Today*, 1993, 26:1:56

Leonhard, K., "Different causative factors in different forms of schizophrenia," lecture delivered at Regional Symposium of the World Psychiatric Association, Rio de Janeiro, 18–21 April 1985

Levi, S., "Ultrasonic assessment of the high rate of human multiple pregnancy in the first trimester," *J. Chi. Ultrasound,* 1976, 4:1:3–5

Levin, M., "Comment on the Minnesota transracial adoption study," *Intelligence,* 1994, 19:13–20

Lewis, E., "Stillbirth: psychological consequences and strategies of management," in Milunsky, A., Friedman, E.A., Cluck, L. (eds), *Advances in Perinatal Medicine, Vol. 3,* New York, Plenum, 1983

Lewis, E. and Bryan, E.M., "Management of perinatal loss of a twin," *British Medical Journal,* 1988, 297:1321–3

Lewis, E. and Bourne, S., "Perinatal death," *Baillière's Clinical Obstetrics and Gynaecology,* 1989, 3:4:935–53

Lewontin, R.C., Rose, S., Kamin, L., *Not in Our Genes: Biology, Ideology, and Human Nature,* New York, Pantheon Books, 1984

Lifton, R.J., *The Nazi Doctors,* New York, Basic Books, 1986

Locke, J.L. and Mather, P.L., "Genetic factors in the ontogeny of spoken language: evidence from monozygotic and dizygotic twins," *J. Child Lang.,* 1989, 16:553–9

Loehlin, J.C., "Heredity, environment, and the structure of the California Psychological Inventory," *Multivariate Behavioral Research,* 1987, 22:137–48

———, "Partitioning, environmental, and genetic contributions to behavioral development," *American Psychologist,* 1989, 44:10:1285–92

———, "Nature, nurture, and conservatism in the Australian twin study," *Behavior Genetics,* 1993, 23:3:287–90

———, "What has behavioral genetics told us about the nature of personality?" in Bouchard Jr., T.J. and Propping, P. (eds), *Twins as a Tool of Behavioral Genetics,* Chichester, John Wiley, 1993

Loehlin, J.C., Horn, J.M., Willerman, L., "Personality resemblance in adoptive families," *Behavior Genetics,* 1981, 11:4: 309–30

———, "Heredity, environment, and IQ in the Texas Adoption Project," in Sternberg, R.J. and Grigorenko, E.L. (eds), *Intelligence: Heredity and Environment,* Cambridge, Cambridge University Press, 1996

Loehlin, J.C., Willerman, L., Horn, J.M., "Personality resemblances between unwed mothers and their adopted-away offspring," *Journal of Personality and Social Psychology,* 1982, 42:6:1089–99

———, "Personality resemblances in adoptive families when the children are late-adolescent or adult," *Journal of Personality and Social Psychology,* 1985, 48:2:376–92

———, "Personality resemblance in adoptive families: a 10-year follow-up," *Journal of Personality and Social Psychology,* 1987, 53:5:961–9

Lord, J.M., "Intra-abdominal fetus in fetu," *J. Path. Bact.,* 1956, 72:627–41

Luke, B., "The changing pattern of multiple births in the United States: maternal and infant characteristics, 1973 and 1990," *Obstetrics and Gynecology,* 1994, 84:1:101–6

Luke, B. and Keith, L.G., "Monozygotic twinning as a congenital defect and congenital defects in monozygotic twins,' *Fetal Diagn. Ther.,* 1990, 5:61–9

Luke, B., Keith, L., Witter, F., "Theoretical model for reducing neonatal morbidity and mortality and associated costs among twins," *Journal of Maternal-Fetal Medicine,* 1992, 1:14–19

Luke, B., Minogue, J., Abbey, H., Keith, L., Witter, F.R., Feng, T.I., Johnson, T.R.B., "The association between maternal weight gain and the birthweight of twins," *Journal of Maternal-Fetal Medicine,* 1992, 1:267–76

Luke, B., Williams, C., Minogue, J., Keith, L., "The changing pattern of infant mortality in the US: the role of prenatal factors and obstetrical implications," *Int. J. Gynecol. Obstet.,* 1993, 40:199–212

Lykken, D., *The Antisocial Personalities,* Mahway, NJ, Lawrence Erlbaum Associates, 1995

Lykken, D.T., Bouchard Jr., T.J., McGue, M., Tellegen, A., "Heritability of interests: a twin study," *Journal of Applied Psychology,* 1993, 78:4:649–61

Lykken, D.T., McGue, M., Tellegen, A., Bouchard Jr., T.J., "Emergenesis: genetic traits that may not run in families," *American Psychologist,* 1992, 47:12:1565–77

Lykken, D.T. and Tellegen, A., "Is human mating adventitious or the result of lawful choice? A twin study of mate selection," *Journal of Personality and Social Psychology,* 1993, 65:1:56–68

Lykken, D.T., Tellegen, A., Lacono, W.G., "EEG spectra in twins: evidence for a neglected mechanism of genetic determination," *Physiological Psychology,* 1982, 10:1:60–5

Lynn, R., "Some reinterpretations of the Minnesota transracial adoption study," *Intelligence,* 1994, 19:21–7

Lyons, M.J., True, W., Eisen, S., et al., "Differential heritability of adult and juvenile antisocial traits, *Arch. Gen. Psychiatry,* 1995, 52:906–915

Lytton, H., Watts, D., Dunn, B.E., "Twin-singleton differences in verbal ability: where do they stem from?" *Intelligence,* 1987, 11:359–69

MacGillvray, I., Campbell, D.M., Thompson, B. (eds), *Twinning and Twins,* Chichester, John Wiley, 1988

McClearn, G.E. and DeFries, J.C. (eds), *Introduction to Behavioral Genetics,* San Francisco, W.H. Freeman, 1973

McClearn, G.E., Johansson, B., Burg, S., "Substantial genetic influence on cognitive abilities in twins 80 or more years old," *Science,* 1997, 276:1560–3

McCrae, R.R. and Costa, Jr, P.T., "Recalled parent-child relations and adult personality," *Journal of Personality,* 1988, 56:2:417–33

McFadden, D., "A masculinizing effect on the auditory systems of human females having male co-twins," *Proc. Natl. Acad. Sci.,* 1993, 90:11900–4

———, "A speculation about the parallel ear asymmetries and sex differences in hearing sensitivity and otoacoustic emissions," *Hearing Research,* 1993, 68:143–51

McFadden, D. and Loehlin, J.C., "On the heritability of spontaneous otoacoustic emissions: a twin study," *Hearing Research,* 1995, 85:1:181–98

McFadden, D. and Mishra, R., "On the relation between hearing sensitivity and otoacoustic emissions," *Hearing Research,* 1993, 71:208–13

McFadden, D. and Pasanen, E.G., "Otoacoustic emissions and quinine sulfate," *J. Acoust. Soc. Am.,* 1994, 95:6:3460–74

McGue, M., "From proteins to cognitions: the behavioral genetics of alcoholism," in Plomin, R. and McClearn, G.E. (eds), *Nature, Nurture, and Psychology,* Washington DC, American Psychological Association, 1993

———, "Genes and behavior," *Scientific American,* 1993, 269:5:8

———, "The democracy of the genes," *Nature,* 31 July 1997, 388, 417–18

McGue, M. and Bouchard Jr., T.J., "Genetic and environmental influences on human behavioral differences," *Annual Review of Neuroscience,* in press

McGue, M., Bouchard Jr., T.J., Iancono, W.G., Lykken, D.T., "Behavioral genetics of cognitive ability: a life-span perspective," in Plomin, R. and McClearn, G.E. (eds), *Nature, Nurture, and Psychology,* Washington DC, American Psychological Association, 1993

McGue, M. and Lykken, D.T., "Genetic influence on risk of divorce," *Psychological Science,* 1992, 3:6:368–73

McGue, M., Pickens, R.W., Svikis, D.S., "Sex and age effects on the inheritance of alcohol problems: a twin study," *Journal of Abnormal Psychology,* 1992, 101:1:3–17

McGue, M., Vaupel, J.W., Holm, N., Harvald, B., "Longevity is moderately heritable in a sample of Danish twins born 1870–1880," *Journal of Gerontology,* 1993, 48:6:B237–44

McGuffin, P. and Katz, R., "The genetics of depression and manic-depressive disorder," *British Journal of Psychiatry,* 1989, 155:294–304

McGuire, J.M., "Twin peaks: six sets of identical St. Louis siblings talk about life as part of a pair," *St. Louis Post-Dispatch,* 7 November 1993

Mackintosh, N.J., *Cyril Burt: Fraud or Framed?* Oxford, Oxford University Press, 1995

Mann, C., "Behavioral genetics in transition: a mass of evidence—animal and human—shows that genes influence behavior, *Science,* 1994, 264:5166:1686

Markow, T.A. and Gottesman, I.I., "Fluctuating dermatoglyphic asymmetry in psychotic twins," *Psychiatric Research,* 1989, 29:1:37–43

Marks, J., "Scientific misconduct: where 'Just say no' fails," *American Scientist,* 1993, 81:380–2

———, "Black, white, other," *Natural History,* December 1994, 32–5

———, *Human Biodiversity: Genes, Race, and History,* Hawthorne, Aldine de Gruyter, 1995

Matheny Jr., A.P., "Injuries among toddlers: contributions from child, mother, and family," *Journal of Pediatric Society,* 1986, 11:2

———, "Children's behavioral inhibition over age and across situations: genetic similarity for a trait during change," *Journal of Personality,* 1989, 57:2:215–35

Matheny, A.P., Riese, M.L., Wilson, R.S., "Rudiments of infant temperament: newborn to 9 months," *Developmental Psychology,* 1985, 21:486–94

Mealey, L. and Segal, N.L., "Heritable and environmental variables affect reproduction-related behaviors, but not ultimate reproductive success," *Person. Individ. Diff.,* 1993, 14:6: 783–94

Mehler, B., "In genes we trust: when science bows to racism," *Reform Judaism,* 1994, 23:2:10–14, 77–9

Metraux, Alfred, *Voodoo in Haiti,* New York, Schocken Books, 1972

Meyer, J.M., Heath, A.C., Eaves, L.J., Mosteller, M., Schienken, R.M., "The predictive power of Cattell's personality questionnaires: an eighteen month prospective study," *Person. Individ. Diff.*, 1988, 9:2:203–12

Miller, E.M., "Prenatal sex hormone transfer: a reason to study opposite-sex twins," *Person. Individ. Diff.*, 1994, 17:4:511–29

Miller, K.L., " 'Twindom' accounts stranger than fiction," *Bucks County Courier,* 5 February 1981

———, "Together Forever," *Life,* April 1996

Minogue, J.P., Tamura, R.K., Keith, L.G., "The Northwestern University Twin Study XV: Rationales for a standard of care in compromised twin pregnancies," *Acta Genet. Med. Gemellol.*, 1990, 39:379–82

Money, J. and Ehrhardt, A., *Man and Woman, Boy and Girl,* Baltimore, Johns Hopkins University Press, 1972

Money, J. and Tucker, P., *Sexual Signatures,* Boston, Little, Brown, 1975

Mushinski, M., "Trends in multiple births," *Statistical Bulletin—Metropolitan Life Insurance Company,* 1994, 75:3:28

Neale, M.C. and Stevenson, J., "Rater bias in the EASI temperament scales: a twin study," *Journals of Personality and Social Psychology,* 1989, 56:1:446–55

Nerlich, A., Wisser, J., Krone, S., "Placental findings in 'vanishing twins,' " *Geburtshilfe Frauenheilkd.*, 1992, 52:4:230–4

Neubauer, P.B., "Infantile sexuality and the developmental point of view," *International Journal of Psychiatry,* 1967, 4:54–6

———, "The life cycle as indicated by the nature of the transference in the psychoanalysis of children," *J. Psycho. Anal.*, 1980, 60:137–44

Neubauer, P.B. and Balzert, C., "Genetics and Psychotherapy," paper presented to the American Academy of Psychoanalysts, Miami, Florida, May 1995

Newman, H.H., Freeman, F.N., Holzinger, K.J., *Twins: A Study of Heredity and Environment,* Chicago, University of Chicago Press, 1966

Newton, W., Keith, L., Keith, D., "The Northwestern University Multihospital Twin Study: IV. Duration of gestation according to fetal sex," *American Journal of Obstetrics and Gynecology,* 1984, 149:6:655–8

Noble, E., *Having Twins,* Boston, Houghton Mifflin, 1990

Onstad, S., Skre, I., Edvardsen, J., Torgersen, S., Kringlen, E., "Mental disorders in first-degree relatives of schizophrenics," *Acta Psychiatr. Scand.,* 1991, 83:395–401

Onstad, S., Skre, I., Torgersen, S., Kringlen, E., "Twin concordance for DSM-III-R schizophrenia," *Acta Psychiatr. Scand.,* 1991, 83:463–7

Pakstis, A., Polesky, H., Scarr, S., Katz, S., "Gene frequency estimates for samples of black and white twins from the Philadelphia metropolitan area," *Human Genetics,* 1978, 43:159–77

Pearlman, E.M., "Separation-individuation, self-concept, and object relations in fraternal twins, identical twins, and singletons," *Journal of Psychology,* 1990, 124:6:619–28

Pedersen, N.L., Gatz, M., Plomin, R., et al., "Individual differences in locus of control during the second half of the life span for identical and fraternal twins reared apart and reared together," *Journal of Gerontology,* 1989, 44:4:100–5

Pedersen, N.L., Lichtenstein, P., Plomin, R., DeFaire, U., McClearn, G.E., Matthews, K.A., "Genetic and environmental influences for type-A-like measures and related traits: a study of twins reared apart and twins reared together," *Psychosomatic Medicine,* 1990, 51:138:428–40

Pedersen, N.L., Plomin, R., McClearn, G.E., Friberg, L., "Neuroticism, extraversion, and related traits in adult twins reared apart and reared together," *Journal of Personality and Social Psychology,* 1988, 55:6:950–7

Phillips, D.I.W., "Twin studies in medical research: can they tell us whether diseases are genetically determined?" *Lancet*, 1993, 341:1008

Pillard, R.C. and Weinrich, J.D., "Evidence of familial nature of male homosexuality," *Archives of General Psychiatry*, 1986, 43:808–12

Piontelli, A., "A study on twins before and after birth," *Int. Rev. Psycho-Anal.*, 1989, 16:413–26

Plomin, R., DeFries, J.C., McClearn, G.E., *Behavioral Genetics, 2nd Edition*, New York, W.H. Freeman, 1990

Plomin, R., Pedersen, N.L., Lichtenstein, P., McClearn, G.E., Nesselroade, J.R., "Genetic influence on life events during the last half of the life span," *Psychology and Aging*, 1990, 5:1:25–30

Plomin, R., Pedersen, N.L., McClearn, G.E., Nesselroade, J.R., Bergeman, C.S., "EAS temperaments during the last half of the life span: twins reared apart and twins reared together," *Psychology and Aging*, 1988, 3:1:43–50

Pool, R., "Evidence for homosexuality gene," *Science*, 1993, 261:5119:291

Poole, E.D., "Roger Pearson: race, intelligence, and bias in academe," *Contemporary Psychology*, 1992, 37:6:604

Powledge, T.M., "The inheritance of behavior in twins," *BioScience*, 1993, 43:420

Price, B., "Primary biases in twin studies," *American Journal of Human Genetics*, 1950, 2, 293–352

Raine, A. and Dunkin, J.J., "The genetic and psychophysiological basis of antisocial behavior: implications for counseling and therapy," *Journal of Counseling and Development*, 1990, 68:637–44

Reddy, K.S., Petersen, M.B., Antonarakis, S.E., Blakemore, K.J., "The vanishing twin: an explanation for discordance between chorionic villus karyotype and fetal phenotype," *Prenat-Diagn.*, 1991, 11:679–84

Regehr, S.M., "The genetic aspects of developmental dyslexia," *Canadian Journal of Behavioral Science,* 1987, 19:3:239–53

Reveley, A.M. and Reveley, M.A., "The relationship of twinning to the familial sporadic distinction in schizophrenia," *J. Psychiat. Res,* 1987, 21:4:515–20

Reveley, M.A., Reveley, A.M., Baldy, R., "Left cerebral hemisphere hypodensity in discordant schizophrenic twins: a controlled study," Arch. Gen. Psychiatry, 1987, 44:625–32

Riese, M.L., "Implications of sex differences in neonatal temperament for early risk and developmental/environmental interactions," *Journal of Genetic Psychology,* 1986, 147:4: 507–13

———, "Size for gestational age and neonatal temperament in full-term and preterm AGA-SGA twin pairs," *Journal of Pediatric Psychology,* 1988, 13.4.521–30

Rodgers, J.L., Rowe, D.C., "IQ similarity in twins, siblings, half-siblings, cousins, and random pairs," *Intelligence,* 1987, 11:199–206

Rosanoff, A.J., Handy, L.M., Plesset, I.R., "The etiology of mental deficiency with special reference to its occurrence in twins: a chapter in the genetic history of human intelligence," *Psychological Monographs,* 1937, 48:1–135

Rose, R.J., "Separated twins: data and their limits," *Science,* 1982, 213:959–60

———, "Genetic and environmental variance in content dimensions of the MMPI," *Journal of Personality and Social Psychology,* 1988, 55:2:302–11

———, "Genes and human behavior," *Annual Review of Psychology,* 1995, 46:625–54

Rose, R.J., Boughman, J.A., Corey, L.A., Nance, W.E., Christian, J.C., Kand, K.K., "Data from kinships of monozygotic twins indicate maternal effects on verbal intelligence," *Nature,* 1980, 283:5745:375–7

Rose, R.J. and Ditto, W.B., "A developmental-genetic analysis of common fears from early adolescence to early adulthood," *Child Development,* 1983, 54:2:361–8

Rose, R.J., Harris, E.L., Christian, J.C., Nance, W.E., "Genetic variation in nonverbal intelligence: data from the kinships of identical twins," *Science,* 1979, 205:1153–5

Rose, R.J. and Kaprio, J., "Frequency of social contact and intrapair resemblance of adult monozygotic cotwins—or does shared experience influence personality after all?," *Behavior Genetics,* 1988, 18:3:309

Rose, R.J., Kaprio, J., Viken, R., Winter, T., Romanov, K., Koskenvuo, M., "Use and abuse of alcohol in adolescence: a population study of Finnish twins at age 16," *Psychiatric Genetics,* 1993, 3:142

Rose, R.J., Kaprio, J., Williams, C.J., Viken, R., Obremski, K., "Social contact and sibling similarity: facts, issues, and red herrings," *Behavior Genetics,* 1990, 20:6:763–78

Rose, R.J., Koskenvuo, M., Kaprio, J., Sarna, S., Langinvainio, H., "Shared genes, shared experiences, and similarity of personality: data from 14,288 adult Finnish twins," *Journal of Personality and Social Psychology,* 1988, 54:1:161–71

Rose, R.J., Uchida, I.A., Christian, J.C., "Placentation effects on cognitive resemblance of adult monozygotes," in *Twin Research 3: Intelligence, Personality, and Development,* New York, Alan R. Liss, 1981

Rose, S., "The rise of neurogenetic determinism," *Nature,* 1995, 373:380–2

Rowe, D.C., "As the twig is bent? The myth of child-rearing influences on personality development," *Journal of Counseling and Development,* 1990, 68: 606–611

Rowe, W., "Predestination, divine foreknowledge, and human freedom," in *Philosophy of Religion, 2nd Edition,* Belmont, Wadsworth, 1993

Roy, A., Segal, N.L., Centerwall, B.S., Robinette, C.D., "Suicide in twins," *Archives of General Psychiatry,* 1991, 48:29–32

Rushton, J.P., Fulkner, D.W., Neale, M.C., Nias, D.K.B., Eysenck, H.J., "Ageing and the relation of aggression, altruism and assertiveness scales to the Eysenck Personality Questionnaire," *Person. Individ. Diff.*, 1989, 10:2:261–3

Rutter, M. and Redshaw, J., "Annotation: growing up as a twin: twin-singleton differences in psychological development," *Journal of Child Psychology and Psychiatry*, 1991, 32:6:885–95

Sakai, L.M., Baker, L.A., Jacklin, C.N., "Sex steroids at birth: genetic and environmental variation and covariation," *Developmental Psychobiology*, 1992, 24:8:559–70

Saltus, R., "They often lag in verbal skills," *Boston Globe*, 11 May 1994

Scarr, S., "Goodness within reach," *New York Times Book Review*, 29 September 1985

———, "Three cheers for behavior genetics: winning the war and losing our identity," *Behavior Genetics*, 1987, 17:219–28

———, "Race and gender as psychological variables: social and ethical issues," *American Psychologist*, 1988, 43:56–9

———, "How genotypes and environments combine: development and individual differences," in Downey, G., Caspi, A., Bolger, N. (eds), *Interacting Systems in Human Development*, New York, Cambridge Press, 1989

———, "Sociobiology: the future," *Contemporary Psychology*, 1990, 35:4:411

———, "Toward a more complete sociobiology," *Contemporary Psychology*, 1990, 35:4:410

———, "Developmental theories for the 1990s: development and individual differences," *Child Development*, 1992, 63:1–19

———, "Biological and cultural diversity: the legacy of Darwin for development," *Child Development*, 1993, 64:1333–53

———, "Comments on Needleman's reply to Scarr," *PSR Quarterly*, 1993, 3:1:48–52

———, "Individuality and community: the contrasting role of the state in family life in the United States and Sweden," *Scandinavian Journal of Psychology*, 37, 93–102

———, "How people make their own environments: implications for parents and policy makers," *Psychology, Public Policy, and Law,* 2, 204–28

———, "Psychological science in the public arena: three cases of dubious influence," *Scandinavian Journal of Psychology,* 36, 164–88

———, "Psychology will be truly evolutionary when behavior genetics is included," *Psychological Inquiry,* 6, 68–71

Scarr, S. and McCartney, K., "How people make their own environment: a theory of genotype—environmental effects," *Child Development,* 1983, 54:424–35

Scarr, S., Pakstis, A., Katz, S., Barker, W., "Absence of a relationship between degree of white ancestry and intellectual skills within a black population," *Human Genetics,* 1977, 39:69–86

Scarr, S. and Ricciuti, A., "What effects do parents have on their children?" in Okagaki, L. and Sternberg, J. (eds), *Directors of Development: Influences on the Development of Children's Thinking,* Hillsdale, Erlbaum, 1991

Scarr, S. and Weinberg, R.A., "IQ test performance of black children adopted by white families," *American Psychologist,* 1976, 31:726–39

———, "The influence of 'family background' on intellectual attainment," *American Sociological Review,* 1978, 43:674–92

———, "The Minnesota adoption studies: genetic differences and malleability," *Child Development,* 1983, 54:260–7

———, "Educational and occupational achievements of brothers and sisters in adoptive and biologically related families," *Behavior Genetics,* 1994, 24:4:301–25

Scarr, S., Weinberg, R.A., Waldman, I.D., "IQ correlations in transracial adoptive families," *Intelligence,* 1993, 17:541–55

Scheinfeld, A., *Twins and Supertwins,* Baltimore, Penguin, 1973

Schneider, K.T.M., Vetter, K., Huch, R., Huch, A., "Acute polyhydramnios complicating twin pregnancies," *Acta Genet. Med. Gemellol.,* 1985, 34:179–84

Schwartz, R.M., Keith, L.G., Keith, D.M., "The Nordic contribution to the English language twin literature," *Acta Obstet. Gynecol. Scand.*, 1986, 65:599–604

Sciarra, J.J. and Keith, L.G., "Multiple pregnancy: an international perspective," *Acta Genet. Med. Gemellol.*, 1990, 39:353–60

Scott, J.P., "Why does human twin research not produce results consistent with those from nonhuman animals?" *Behavior and Brain Sciences*, 1987, 10:1:39–40

Segal, N.L., "The nature vs. nurture laboratory," *Twins*, July/August 1984, 56–7

———, "Zygosity testing laboratory and the investigator's judgment," *Acta Genet. Med. Gemellol.*, 1984, 33:515–21

———, "Holocaust twins: their special bond," *Psychology Today*, August 1985

———, "ESP: does it exist in twins?" *Twins*, November/ December 1986, 28–9, 55

———, "Twin studies: a brief overview," in Macdonald, K.B. (ed), *Sociobiological Perspectives on Human Development*, New York, Springer-Verlag, 1988

———, "Origins and implications of handedness and relative birth weight for IQ in monozygotic twin pairs," *Neuropsychologist*, 1989, 27:4:549–61

———, "The importance of twin studies for individual differences research," *Journal of Counseling and Development*, 1990, 68:612–22

———, "Twin Research at Auschwitz-Birkenau: implications for the use of Nazi data today," in Caplan, A. (ed), *When Medicine Went Mad*, Ottowa, Humana Press, 1992

———, "Twins (human)," in *Encyclopedia of Science and Technology, Vol. 18*, New York, McGraw-Hill, 1992

———, "Implications of twin research for legal issues involving young twins," *Law & Human Behavior*, 1993, 17:1:43–57

———, "SURPs: not exactly twins, but. . ." *Twins*, November/December 1993, 54–6

———, "Twin, sibling, and adoption methods: tests of evolutionary hypotheses," *American Psychologist,* 1993, 48:9: 43–56

———, "Letters to the editor," *Developmental and Behavioral Pediatrics,* 1994, 15:2:146

———, "Mourning my best friend," *Twins,* September/October 1994, 22–3, 31

———, " 'They're identical? No way!' " *Twins,* November/December 1994, 27–9

———, "What families of identical females need to know," *Twins,* July/August 1995, 37–9

Segal, N.L. and Bouchard Jr., T.J., "Grief intensity following the loss of a twin and other relatives: test of kinship genetic hypothesis," *Human Biology,* 1993, 65:1:87–105

Segal, N.L., Dysken, M.W., Bouchard Jr., T.J., Pedersen, N.L., Eckert, E.D., Heston, L.L., "Tourette's disorder in a set of reared-apart triplets: genetic and environmental influences," *Am. J. Psychiatry,* 1990, 147:2:196–9

Segal, N.L. and Russell, J., "IQ similarity in monozygotic and dizygotic twin children: effects of the same versus different examiners: a research note," *J. Child. Psychol. Psychiat.,* 1991, 32:4:703–8

———, "Twins in the classroom: school policy issues and recommendations," *Journal of Educational and Psychological Consultation,* 1992, 3:69–84

Seligman, D., "A substantial inheritance: burgeoning evidence shows that genetic factors play a great role in many human potentials and tendencies," *National Review,* 1994, 46:19:56

Shields, J., "Personality differences and neurotic traits in normal twin schoolchildren: a study in psychiatric genetics," *Eugenics Review,* 1954, 45:213–46

———, *Monozygotic Twin: Brought Up Apart and Brought Up Together: an Investigation into the Genetic and Environmental Causes of Variation in Personality,* London, Oxford University Press, 1962

——, "MZA twins: their use and abuse," in *Twin Research: Psychology and Methodology,* New York, Alan R. Liss, 1978

Silverman, M.A., Rees, K., Neubauer, P.B., "On a central psychic constellation," *Psychoanalytic Study of the Child,* 1975, 30:127–57

Skinner, B.F., "Pigeons in a pelican," *American Psychologist,* 1960, 15:28–37

Skovholt, T.M., "Counseling implications of genetic research: a dialogue with Thomas Bouchard," *Journal of Counseling and Development,* 1990, 68:633–6

Smith, C., "Twins' mysterious speech has many experts talking," *San Diego Union,* 31 July 1977

Stafford, L., "Maternal input to twin and singleton children: implications for language," *Human Communication Research,* 1987, 13:4:429–62

Stan, S. and Huffman, D., "The 'Jim twins:' a mirror image after 39 years apart," *Us, 1 May 1979*

Stassen, H.H., Lykken, D.T., Bomben, G., "The within-pair EEG similarity of twins reared apart," *European Archives of Psychiatry and Neurological Sciences,* 1988, 237:244–52

Stassen, H.H., Lykken, D.T., Propping, P., Bomben, G., "Genetic determination of the human EEG," *Human Genetics,* 1988, 80:165–76

Stern, C., *Principles of Human Genetics, 3rd Edition,* San Francisco, W.H. Freeman, 1973

Stevenson, J. and Fielding, J., "Ratings of temperament in families of young twins," *British Journal of Developmental Psychology,* 1985, 3:143–52

Stevenson, J. and Fredman, G., "The social environmental correlates of reading ability," *J. Child Psychol. Psychiat.,* 1990, 31:5:681–98

Stevenson, J., Graham, P., Fredman, G., McLoughlin, V., "A twin study of genetic influences on reading and spelling ability and disability," *Child Psychology and Psychiatry,* 1987, 28:2:229–47

Suematsu, H., Kuboki, T., Ogata, E., "Anorexia nervosa in monozygotic twins," *Psychother. Psychosom.*, 1986, 45:46–50

Sulloway, F., *Born to Rebel*, New York, Pantheon Books, 1996

Swan, G.E., LaRue, A., Carmelli, D., et al., "Decline in cognitive performance in aging twins' heritability and biobehavioral predictors from the National Heart, Lung and Blood Institute Twin Study," *Archives of Neurology*, 1992, 49:476–81

Szajnberg, N.M., Skrinjaric, J., Moore, A., "Affect attunement, attachment, temperament, and zygosity: a twin study," *J. Am. Acad. Child Adolesc. Psychiatry*, 1989, 28:2:249–53

Tambs, K., Sundet, J.M., Eaves, L., Berg, K., "Relations between EPQ and Jenkins activity survey," *Person. Individ. Diff.*, 1989, 10:12:1229–35

Tambs, K., Sundet, J.M., Magnu, P., Berg, K., "No recruitment bias for questionnaire data related to IQ in classical twin studies," *Person. Individ. Diff.*, 1987, 10:2:269–71

Tanimura, M., Matsui, I., Kobayashi, N., "Child abuse of one of a pair of twins in Japan," *Lancet*, 1990, 336:8726:1298

Tellegen, A., Lykken, D.T., Bouchard Jr., T.J., Wilcox, K.J., Segal, N.L., Rich, S., "Personality similarity in twins reared apart and together," *Journal of Personality and Social Psychology*, 54, 1031–1039, 1988

Thomas, A. and Chess, S., *Temperament and Development*, New York, Brunner/Mazel, 1977

Thomas, A., Chess, S., Birch, H.C., Hertzig, M.E., Korn, S., *Behavioral Individuality in Early Childhood*, New York, New York University Press, 1971

Torgersen, S., "Comorbidity of major depression and anxiety disorders in twin pairs," *Am. J. Psychiatry*, 1990, 147:9:1199–202

Torrey, E.F., "Stalking the schizovirus," *Schizophrenia Bulletin*, 1988, 14:2:223–9

———, "Offspring of twins with schizophrenia," *Arch. Gen. Psychiatry*, 1990, 47:976–8

U.S. Department of Health and Human Services, "State-specific variation in rates of twin births—United States, 1992–1994," *Morbidity and Mortality Weekly Report,* 1997, 46:6:121–5

Vagero, D. and Leon, D., "Ischaemic heart disease and low birth weight: a test of the fetal-origins hypothesis from the Swedish Twin Registry," *Lancet,* 1994, 343:8892:260

Vernon, P.A., "The heritability of measures of speed of information-processing," *Person. Individ. Diff.,* 1989, 10:5:573–6

Viken, R.J., Rose, R.J., Kaprio, J., Koskenvuo, M., "A developmental genetic analysis of adult personality: extraversion and neuroticism from 18 to 59 years of age," *Journal of Personality and Social Psychology,* 1994, 66:4:722–30

Vogel, F. and Motulsky, A.G., *Human Genetics: Problems and Approaches,* Berlin, Springer-Verlag, 1979

Volpe, E., *Biology and Human Concerns, 4th Edition,* Dubuque, Wm. C. Brown, 1993

Wade, N., "IQ and heredity: suspicion of fraud beclouds classic experiment," *Science,* 1976, 194:916–19

Waldman, I.D., Weinberg, R.A., Scarr, S., "Racial-group differences in IQ in the Minnesota Transracial Adoption Study: a reply to Levin and Lynn," *Intelligence,* 1994, 19:29–44

Waller, N.G., Kojetin, B.A., Bouchard Jr., T.J., Lykken, D.T., Tellegen, A., "Genetic and environmental influences on religious interests, attitudes, and values: a study of twins reared apart and together," *Psychological Science,* 1990, 1:2:138–42

Waller, N. and Shaver, P., "The importance of nongenetic influences on romantic love styles: a twin-family study," *Psychological Science,* 1994, 5:268–74

Watson, J.B., *Behaviorism,* New York, Norton Library, 1970

Watson, P., *Twins: An Uncanny Relationship,* New York, Viking Press, 1981

Weinberg, R.A., Scarr, S., Waldman, I.D., "The Minnesota Transracial Adoption Study: a follow-up of IQ test performance at adolescence," *Intelligence,* 1992, 16:117–35

Welsh, E., "At home: a bond stronger than many marriages," *Daily Telegraph,* 5 February 1994

Whitfield, K.E. and Miles, T.P., "Studying ethnicity and behavioral medicine: a quantitative genetic approach," in Turner, J.R., Cardon, L.R., Hewitt, J.K. (eds), *Behavior Genetic Approaches in Behavioral Medicine,* New York, Plenum Press, 1995

Wiesel, T., "Genetics and Behavior," *Science,* 1994, 264:1647

Willerman, L., Loehlin, J.C., Horn, J.M., "An adoption and a cross-fostering study of the Minnesota Multiphasic Personality Inventory (MMPI) psychopathic deviate scale," *Behavior Genetics,* 1992, 22:5:515–29

Williams, R. and Medalie, J.H., "Twins: double pleasure or double trouble?" *American Family Physician,* 1994, 49:869

Wilson, R.S., "Synchronies in mental development: an epigenetic perspective," *Science,* 1978, 202:939–48

———, "Risk and resilience in early mental development,," *Developmental Psychology,* 1985, 21:795–805

Wilson, R.S. and Matheny, Jr, A.P., "Behavior-genetics research in infant temperament: the Louisville twin study," in Plomin, R. and Dunn, J. (eds) *The Study of Temperament: Changes, Continuities and Challenges,* Hillsdale, Lawrence Erlbaum, 1986

Woodward, J., "The bereaved twin," *Acta Genet. Med. Gemellol.,* 1988, 37:173–80

Yates, N. and Brash, H. "An investigation of the physical and mental characteristics of a pair of like twins reared apart from infancy," *Annals of Eugenics,* 1941, 11:89–101

Yoe, M.R., "Twin Peeks," *University of Chicago Magazine,* 1990, 82:4:22–5

Zerbin-Rudin, E., "Psychiatric genetics and psychiatric nosology," *J. Psychiat. Res.,* 1987, 21:4:377–83

Index

Acardia, 113
Adoption studies
  and family environment, 136–138
  and IQ, 62–63
  placing identical twins, 39–40
  separation of twins, 1, 2–3
  vs. twin studies, 135
Age. *See* Identical twins, similarity over time
Aggression, as genetic expression, 82
Alcoholism, and identical twins, 80–81, 154
American Breeders' Association, 15
Amy and Beth case, 1, 2, 3–6
Anastomoses, 113
Ando, Juko, 68
Animals, polyzygotic offspring, 11
Antisocial behavior
  criminality, 64–65, 123, 132–133
  environmental factors, 132–133
  heritability of, 64–65, 123
Auschwitz, and twin studies, 17–21

Bailey, Michael, 81–82
Baker, Laura, 128
Behavioral genetics. *See also* Heritability
  criticism of, 31, 71–72, 78–79
  vs. environmentalism, 122
  as field of study, 8
  historical basis of field, 12
  influence of, 143–144
  and intelligence, 72–75, 79, 144, 145
  and personality, 146–148
  resurgence of, 10, 148
  and social policy, 9–10, 132, 148–149
  statistical studies, 78–79
  test subjects, 148
  view of environment, 147, 148–149
Behaviorism, rise of, 22–23. *See also* Environment
The Bell Curve, 13, 30, 75
Bernard, Viola W., 39–40, 41
Beth and Amy case. *See* Amy and Beth case
Binet, Alfred, 144
Biological determinism, 78. *See also* Behavioral genetics
Birth defect, occurrence of twins as, 11, 86, 96
Black Elderly Twin Study, 7
Blackmore, Susan, 59
Blacks. *See* Race
Boklage, Charles E.
  and chimeras, 94
  and mirror imaging, 119
  study of schizophrenia in identical twins, 120–121
  study of twins *vs.* singletons, 97
  view of vanishing twins, 88–89
Bouchard, Thomas J., Jr., 43–57, 58, 61, 62, 63, 141
British class system, 14
Bryan, Elizabeth, 91
Bunker brothers, 118
Burn, John, 105, 107–108, 109, 110

Burt, Sir Cyril
  corroboration of findings, 61
  defenders of, 32–33
  exposé of, 31–32
  study of heritability of intelligence, 26–28

Calico cats, 106
Cancer, and twins, 123–124
Central Intelligence Agency, 59–60
Chimeras, 94–95, 96
Choice. *See* Free will
Chromosomes
  and "gay gene," 81–82
  and muscular dystrophy, 106–107, 108
  and twinning, 106, 108–110
Chronic disease, and twins, 124
Classic twin method, 12–14, 18, 19
Cloning
  kinship issues, 85–86
  methods, 85
  vs. twinning process, 86
Communism, and twin studies, 15–16
Conjoined twins. *See* Siamese twins
Conservatism *vs.* liberalism, 9–10, 147–148
Contract with America, 10
Conway, J., 31–32
Criminality, 64–65, 123, 132–133. *See also* Violent behavior
Cystic fibrosis, 95, 96. *See also* Birth defect, occurrence of twins as

Daniels, Michael, 74
Depression, in female twins, 140, 141
Derom, Catherine, 98
Determinism, 78. *See also* Behavioral genetics
Devlin, Bernie, 73, 74, 75
Diamond, Milton, 116, 117
Divorce
  environmental factors, 150, 151–152
  heritability of, 150–151, 152
  and identical twins, 150–151, 154
Dizygotic (DZ) twins. *See* Fraternal twins
Dopamine, 80
Duchenne disease, 106, 107
DZ (dizygotic) twins. *See* Fraternal twins

Eaves, Lindon J., 155–157
Education, 28–30. *See also* Intelligence
Ehrhardt, Anke A., 114
Embryos. *See* Chimeras
Environment
  vs. behavioral genetics, 122, 148–150
  and criminality, 65, 123, 132–133
  and free will issue, 154–157
  as heritable factor, 140
  and intelligence, 72–75, 144–145
  and race, 134–138
  role in personality development, 147
Eugenics
  coinage of term, 14
  as movement, 14–15, 145
  and Nazis, 16–22
Extrasensory perception, 59–60
Extraversion, 127–128, 129, 146
Eysenck, Hans, 146

Families, role of shared environment, 62, 141
Farber, Susan, 69
Fertility drugs, 102
Festival of twins, 8–9, 92, 121
Fetus-in-fetu, 89–90
Fisk, Nicholas, 111–112
Fletcher, Ronald, 32
Follicle-stimulating hormone (FSH), 99, 100, 101–102
Fragile X syndrome, 108
Fraternal twins
  differences between, 96–97
  how they occur, 11–12, 96, 98–99
  vs. identical twins, 96, 97–99
  vs. ordinary siblings, 75
  prevalence of, 99–101
Free will, 144, 154, 155–156
Fries, Charles, 23

Galland, Eddie, 37, 39
Galton, Sir Francis

corroboration of findings, 63
study of twins, 12–14, 15, 144
"Gay gene," 81–82. *See also* Homosexuality
Gedda, Luigi, 120
Gender. *See also* Homosexuality; Transsexuals
and identical twins, 113–117
John/Joan case, 114–117
Genes. *See also* Heritability; Behavioral genetics
vs. behavior, 22, 83
and free will issue, 154–157
and intelligence, 72–75, 79, 144–145
and race, 28–30, 134–138
role in personality development, 147
Genome, human, 79
Giggle sisters, 50–51
Gillie, Oliver, 31
Golbin, Alexander, 121
Golbin, Irene, 121
Gonadotrophic hormones, 101–102
Goodship, Daphne, 50–51
Goodship, Judith, 109
Great Society, 10

Hall, Jerry L., 85
Hall, Judith, 95, 98, 113
Handwriting, and twins, 13
Happiness, and twins, 127–129
Hearnshaw, Leslie, 32
Heart defects, 96, 107–108
Height, heritability of, 25–26, 29
Hensel sisters, 119
Herbert, Barbara, 50–51
Heritability. *See also* Behavioral genetics
and behavioral characteristics, 147–148
and criminality, 64–65, 123
defined, 24
of environment itself, 140
and height, 25–26, 29
and intelligence, 26–34, 73–75, 79, 144–145
measuring, 25
Hermaphrodites, 95
Herrnstein, Richard J., 13, 30, 134
Homosexuality, 52, 81–82, 122
Howard, Margaret, 31–32
Human genome, 79

Identical twins
and alcoholism, 80–81, 154
Amy and Beth, 1, 2, 3–6
circumstances of separation, 68–69
vs. cloning, 86
conjoined, 118–119
differences between, 110–122
and divorce, 150–151, 154
fascination with, 6, 11, 37–38, 56–57, 110
vs. fraternal twins, 96, 97–99
gay members, 52, 81–82, 122
Giggle sisters, 50–51
handwriting, 13
and heart defects, 96, 107–108
how they occur, 11–12, 99
Jack and Oskar, 53–55
Jim twins, 43–48, 76–77
left-handedness of, 86, 94, 96, 119, 120
life before birth, 89–91
love life, 124–127
mirror imaging, 13, 119–121
mixed gender, 113–117
and parental warmth, 152–153
physical resemblance, 72
placing for adoption, 1, 2–3, 39–40
prevalence of, 102–103
psychic connections, 56, 58–60
question of selfhood, 157–160
role of shared family environment, 62, 141
schizophrenia in, 120–121
separated *vs.* raised together, 62, 70
and shared genetic traits, 60–61, 110
shared *vs.* non-shared environment, 62, 140–142, 147–148
similarity over time, 70, 73, 74
stories of reuniting, 37–39, 76
studying. *See* Twin studies
timing of split, 117–119
trading lives, 157–160
as type of birth defect, 11, 86, 96

Inherited tendencies. *See* Heritability
Intelligence. *See also* IQ scores
  Burt studies, 27–28
  environmental factors, 72–75, 144, 145
  measuring. *See* IQ scores
  question of heritability, 26–34, 73–75, 79, 144–145
  and race, 28–30, 133–138
  and twin studies, 31, 73, 74–75
In vitro fertilization, 85, 102
IQ scores. *See also* Intelligence
  adoption studies, 62–63
  Burt studies, 27–28
  and illegitimacy, 131–132
  origin of tests, 144–145
  and race, 28–29, 133–138
  reliability of statistical correlations, 78
  and twin studies, 7–8, 68, 69, 71, 72

Jensen, Arthur R., 28–29, 30, 32, 134
Jim twins, 43–48, 76–77
John/Joan case, 115–117
Johnson, Robert B., 32
Jordan, David Starr, 14–15

Kamin, Leon
  as behaviorist, 31, 78, 79
  as critic of behavior genetics, 31, 71–72
  as critic of Burt, 30–31, 32
  as critic of twin studies, 31, 67–68, 69, 72, 76
Keith, Donald, 92, 93, 121, 125–126
Keith, Louis, 90, 92, 102, 121, 125–126
Kellman, Claire, 35–36, 41
Kellman, David, 35–36, 38–39
Kellman, Richard, 35–36
Kendler, Kenneth S., 140, 141

Left-handedness, in twins, 86, 94, 96, 119, 120
Lewis, James, 44, 46–48
Lewis, Jess and Lucille, 43
Lewis, Lucille, 43, 44
Lewontin, Richard C., 71, 77, 78
Liberalism *vs.* conservatism, 9–10, 22, 147–148
Lifton, Robert Jay, 18
Lone Twin Network, 91
Louisville Twin Study, 72
Love life of twins, 124–127
Lush, J. L., 24
Lykken, David, 58–59, 60, 71, 124, 125, 126–127, 131–132, 151
Lyons, M. J., 65
Lysenko, T. D., 15–16

Mack, Thomas, 123
Mackintosh, N.J., 33
Markuson, Phyllis, 125–126
Marxism, and twin studies, 15–16
Masha and Dasha, 118
Maternal effect, 74, 75, 76
McCartney, Kathleen, 139
McClearn, Gerald, 65, 73
McGue, Matt, 124, 151
Mengele, Josef, 17–21
Mental abilities. *See* Intelligence
Mill, John Stuart, 13
Minnesota, University of. *See also* Bouchard, Thomas J., Jr.; Lykken, David
  funding twin studies, 57
  twin registry, 7
  twin study process, 48–50
Mirror imaging, 13, 119–121
Money, John, 114, 115, 116
Monozygotic (MZ) twins. *See* Identical twins
Moynihan, Daniel Patrick, 77–78
Multiple births, prevalence of, 99–101
Multiple Births Foundation, 91
Murray, Charles, 13
Muscular dystrophy, 105, 106–107, 108
MZ (monozygotic) twins. *See* Identical twins

Nature *vs.* nurture. *See also* Heritability
  in aspects of human development, 146–148

as false dichotomy, 139
and free will issue, 154–157
question of percentages, 24
role of twin studies, 1, 2–3, 7–10
Nazis, twin studies, 16–22, 64, 123
Neubauer, Peter, 1–2, 7, 36, 39, 40–41
Neuroticism, 128, 129, 146
Non-shared *vs.* shared environment, 62, 140–142, 147–148
Nyiszli, Miklos, 21

Ohio, festival of twins, 8–9, 92, 121

Pakstis, Andrew, 135
Parents
adoptive *vs.* biological, 137–138
licensing idea, 131–133
psychiatric patients as, 153
rating warmth of, 152–153
Pauling, Linus, 8
Personality
heritability of, 147
measuring, 15, 70, 146–147
and twin studies, 48–49
Pillard, Richard C., 82
Pioneer Fund, 57
Plomin, Robert, 79
Programmed instruction, 24
Psychoticism, 146–147

Race
Black Elderly Twin Study, 7
cultural disadvantages *vs.* genetic differences, 134–138
and heritability of intelligence, 13, 14, 28–30
and IQ scores, 28–29, 133–138
Registries of twins, 7, 146
Religion, and twins raised apart, 57–58, 146
Reuniting of identical twins, 37–39, 76
Roeder, Katherine, 74
Rose, Richard, 118
Rose, Steven, 71, 78
Scarr, Sandra, 62–63, 133–138, 141–142, 151–152

Schizophrenia, 120–121
Segal, Nancy, 111, 120
Selfhood, and identical twins, 157–160
Sex. *See* Homosexuality; Love life of twins
Shafran, Robert, 36–37, 38–39
Shared *vs.* non-shared environment, 62, 140–142, 147–148
Shields, James, 67
Siamese twins, 90, 118–119
Sigmundson, H. Keith, 116
Skinner, B.F., 23–24, 30
Social attitudes, heritability of, 123, 147
Social programs, views of need, 9–10, 148
Southern California Twin Project, 128
Soviet Union, and twin studies, 15–16
Spencer, Herbert, 14
Spina bifida, 96
Spock, Benjamin, 23
Springer, Ernest and Sarah, 43
Springer, James, 43–44, 46–48
Statistics, criticism of correlation, 77
Stohr, Oskar, 53, 54–55

Teeth, and twins, 97
Tellegen, Auge, 126–127
Teplica, David, 92–94
Teratomas, 89, 90
Tourette's syndrome, 79–80
Trading lives, 159–160
Transsexuals, 114–117
Triplets restaurant, 39
Tucker, Elizabeth, 108
Turner's syndrome, 114
Twin registries, 7, 146
Twins. *See also* Identical twins; Fraternal twins
Amy and Beth, 1, 2, 3–6
annual festival, 8–9, 92, 121
fraternal *vs.* identical, 96, 97–99
handwriting, 13
how they occur, 11–12, 98–99
Jack and Oskar, 53–55
Jim twins, 43–48, 76–77
left-handedness in, 86, 94, 96, 119, 120

Twins (*cont'd.*)
  life before birth, 89–91
  mirror-image, 13, 119–121
  prevalence of, 87, 99–103
  registries of, 7, 146
  studying. *See* Twin studies
  third type, 97–98
  threats to early life, 89
  as type of birth defect, 11, 86, 96
  vanished, 87–89, 91–92, 120
  as Vietnam veterans, 153–154
  and X-inactivation, 106, 108–109
Twinsburg, Ohio, 8
Twins (movie), 111
Twin studies. *See also* Galton, Sir Francis
  academic warfare over, 33–34
  vs. adoption studies, 135
  Amy and Beth, 1, 2, 3–6
  background, 7, 25
  Bouchard studies, 43–57, 58, 61, 62, 63, 141
  Burt studies, 26–28
  classic twin method, 12–14
  and communism, 15–16
  criticism of, 67–77
  divorce, 150–151, 154
  heritability of intelligence, 26–34, 73–75, 79, 144–145
  Jack and Oskar, 53–55
  Jim twins, 43–48, 76–77
  and Nazis, 16–22, 64, 123
  politics of, 14, 15–16
  racial minorities, 133–138
  schizophrenia, 120–121
  in Soviet Union, 15–16
  third type of twinning, 97–98
  triplets adoption case, 35–41
  twins raised apart, 1, 2–3, 7–10, 27–28, 31, 33, 43–57, 58, 61, 62, 63, 76–77, 83, 141, 146, 154

U.S. Central Intelligence Agency, 59–60
U.S. Veterans Administration, 7

Vanished twins, 87–89, 91–92, 120
Vasilet, Feydor, 100
Verschuer, Count Otmar von, 16–17, 18, 20
Veterans Administration, 7
Vietnam veterans, twins as, 153–154
Violent behavior, 82
Virginia, twin studies, 7, 155
Voodoo culture, 94

Watson, John B., 22
Weinberg, Richard A., 62–63, 135–136
Weinberger, Daniel, 80
Wilmut, Ian, 85
Wise (Louise) Services, 35–36, 38
Womack, Sarah, 100

X chromosomes
  and "gay gene," 81–82
  and muscular dystrophy, 106–107, 108
  and twinning, 106, 108–109
X-inactivation, 106, 108–109

Yoruba tribe, 99
Yufe, Jack, 53–55

Zygosity, 11–12, 40, 95, 118